THE PSYCHOLOGY OF MONEY

Dr. Maxwell Shimba

Shimba Publishing, LLC.

Printed in the United States of America

SHIMBA
PUBLISHING

TABLE OF CONTENTS

PREFACE

By Dr. Maxwell Shimba

Money often plays a leading role in the intricate dance of daily life. It shapes our decisions, influences our relationships, and even determines our sense of security and happiness. Yet, despite its pervasive presence, many of us navigate our financial journeys without fully understanding the psychological underpinnings that drive our financial behaviors. This book, "The Psychology of Money: Unveiling the Secrets of Financial Behavior," aims to shed light on these underlying mechanisms, offering insights that can transform how we manage our finances and, ultimately, our lives.

As a theologian and financial educator, I have spent years studying not only the economic principles that govern wealth but also the human behaviors and mindsets that influence our financial decisions. Throughout my career, I have encountered countless individuals who struggle with money, not due to a lack of resources or intelligence, but because of the psychological barriers and misconceptions that cloud their judgment. It became clear to me that addressing these psychological aspects is just as crucial as understanding the numbers and strategies of finance.

This book is a culmination of my years of research, teaching, and personal experience. It explores the full spectrum of financial behavior, from budgeting and saving to investing and wealth preservation. Each chapter delves into a different aspect of financial psychology, providing practical strategies alongside theoretical insights to help you develop a healthier, more effective relationship with money.

One of the fundamental themes we explore is the distinction between a scarcity mindset and an abundance mindset. How we perceive the availability of resources can drastically affect our financial behavior. By shifting from a mindset of scarcity, where we believe there is never enough, to one of abundance, where we see opportunities and possibilities, we can unlock new paths to financial stability and growth.

We also delve into practical budgeting strategies, such as zero-based budgeting and the 50/30/20 rule, which offer structured approaches to managing your finances. These methods are designed to provide clarity and control, ensuring that every dollar is purposefully directed toward your financial goals.

Understanding cognitive biases and emotional influences is another critical component of this book. These psychological factors often lead to irrational financial decisions, such as impulsive spending or overly conservative investments. By recognizing and addressing these biases, you can make more rational, informed choices that align with your long-term objectives.

Furthermore, this book examines the impact of social and cultural factors on financial behavior. Our family background, societal norms, and cultural values all play a significant role in shaping our attitudes toward money. By understanding these influences, you can develop a more conscious approach to your financial decisions.

As we move towards the conclusion, the book emphasizes the importance of financial education and continuous learning. In an ever-evolving financial landscape, staying informed and adaptable is key to achieving financial success. This book provides a roadmap for lifelong financial literacy, equipping you with the knowledge and tools to navigate your financial journey with confidence.

I invite you to embark on this journey with an open mind and a willingness to explore new perspectives. Whether you are just starting out on your financial path or seeking to refine your existing strategies, "The Psychology of Money" offers valuable insights and practical guidance to help you achieve your financial goals.

Thank you for allowing me to be a part of your financial journey. May this book serve as a catalyst for positive change, empowering you to take control of your finances and create a prosperous, fulfilling future.

Dr. Maxwell Shimba

DR. MAXWELL SHIMBA

CHAPTER 01

INTRODUCTION TO THE PSYCHOLOGY OF MONEY

Understanding Money Beyond Economics

Money is more than a mere medium of exchange or a measure of value; it is a powerful force that profoundly shapes human behavior, society, and economies. To understand money is to understand a significant part of human life. The way people think about, use, and manage money is influenced by a complex interplay of cognitive, emotional, and social factors. These factors shape not only individual financial decisions but also collective economic outcomes.

The Significance of Financial Psychology

Financial psychology is a field that combines principles from psychology and economics to understand how people make financial decisions. It seeks to answer questions such as: Why do people save or spend money the way they do? What influences their investment choices? How do emotions like fear and greed impact financial markets? By delving into the psychology behind financial decisions, we can gain profound insights into human behavior and develop strategies to improve financial well-being.

Cognitive Factors in Financial Behavior

Cognitive factors refer to the mental processes involved in gaining knowledge and comprehension, including aspects such as awareness, perception, reasoning, and judgment. These cognitive processes play a critical role in financial decision-making. For instance, cognitive biases, which are systematic patterns of deviation from norm or rationality in judgment, can significantly impact financial decisions. Common cognitive biases include:

- Overconfidence: The tendency to overestimate one's knowledge or abilities, which can lead to risky financial behaviors such as overtrading or underestimating risks.

- Anchoring: The reliance on the first piece of information encountered (the "anchor") when making decisions, which can lead to inappropriate financial judgments.

- Loss Aversion: The tendency to prefer avoiding losses rather than acquiring equivalent gains, leading to conservative investment strategies or irrational decisions to hold onto losing assets.

Emotional Influences on Financial Decisions

Emotions play a critical role in financial behavior. Financial decisions are often driven by feelings of fear, greed, joy, and regret. For instance:

- Fear and Greed: These emotions can drive market trends and lead to phenomena such as bubbles and crashes. Fear can lead to panic selling, while greed can drive speculative buying.

- Joy and Regret: Positive emotions like joy can lead to increased spending and investment, while regret over past financial decisions can influence future behavior, often leading to risk aversion or overly cautious strategies.

Understanding the role of emotions in financial behavior can help individuals and financial professionals develop better strategies for managing emotional influences and making more rational financial decisions.

Social and Cultural Factors

Social and cultural factors also significantly influence financial behavior. These factors include:

- Family Background: Financial attitudes and behaviors are often learned from family members. Parents' attitudes toward money, spending habits, and investment choices can profoundly influence their children's financial behavior.

- Societal Norms: Social expectations and cultural values shape how individuals perceive and use money. For example, in some cultures, there may be a strong emphasis on saving and frugality, while in others, spending and consumption may be more highly valued.

- Peer Influence: The behavior of peers can also impact financial decisions. Social comparison and the desire to keep up with peers can lead to financial behaviors such as overspending or risky investments.

The Evolution of Financial Behavior

Financial behavior has evolved over time, influenced by changes in economic systems, technological advancements, and shifts in societal values. From the barter systems of ancient societies to the complex financial markets of today, the way people interact with money has changed dramatically. Understanding this evolution can provide valuable context for studying contemporary financial behavior.

The Importance of Financial Education

Financial literacy is crucial for making informed financial decisions. However, many people lack basic financial knowledge, which can lead to poor financial decisions and negative outcomes. Financial education can help individuals understand key financial concepts, develop better money management skills, and make more informed decisions. This chapter will explore the importance of financial education and its role in improving financial behavior and outcomes.

The Future of Financial Behavior

The field of financial behavior is continually evolving. Emerging trends and technologies, such as financial technology (fintech) and artificial intelligence (AI), are transforming the financial landscape and influencing how people interact with money. Understanding these trends and their potential impact on financial behavior is essential for navigating the future of finance.

Conclusion

The psychology of money is a fascinating and complex field that offers valuable insights into human behavior and financial decision-making. By exploring the cognitive, emotional, and social factors that influence financial behavior, we can develop a deeper understanding of the role money plays in our lives and make better financial decisions. This book aims to provide a comprehensive overview of the psychology of money, offering practical strategies and insights to help readers improve their financial well-being.

CHAPTER 02

THE HISTORY AND EVOLUTION OF MONEY

The concept of money is deeply embedded in human history and society. Understanding its evolution is crucial to grasping the psychological impact it has on individuals and communities. This chapter traces the journey of money from primitive barter systems to modern digital currencies, exploring how each transformation has influenced human behavior and societal structures.

The Barter System: The Beginning of Trade

Before the invention of money, people relied on the barter system to exchange goods and services. Barter involves trading items of perceived equal value directly. For example, a farmer might trade a bushel of wheat for a carpenter's services. While barter was functional in small, simple economies, it had significant limitations:

- Double Coincidence of Wants: For a barter exchange to occur, both parties need to want what the other offered, making trades cumbersome and inefficient.

- Lack of Standardized Value: Determining the value of goods was subjective and often led to disputes.

- Indivisibility of Goods: Some goods could not be easily divided to match the value of other goods, complicating exchanges.

The Emergence of Commodity Money

To overcome the limitations of barter, societies began using commodity money—items with intrinsic value that could be used in trade. Examples include:

- Livestock and Grain: Early forms of money in agricultural societies.

- Precious Metals: Gold, silver, and copper were valued for their scarcity, durability, and divisibility. These metals became widely accepted as a medium of exchange.

Commodity money had several advantages:

- Standardized Value: Items like gold and silver had widely recognized value, facilitating trade.

- Portability: Precious metals were easier to transport than bulky goods.

- Divisibility: Metals could be melted and divided into smaller units.

The Invention of Coinage

Around 600 BCE, the Lydians in modern-day Turkey are credited with creating the first standardized coins. These coins were made from electrum, a natural alloy of gold and silver, and were stamped with official symbols to guarantee their value.

The invention of coinage brought several key benefits:

- Uniformity: Standardized coins with guaranteed value made transactions more straightforward.

- Trust: Official stamps on coins reduced the risk of fraud.

- Widespread Acceptance: Coins were more easily accepted across different regions and cultures.

The Development of Paper Money

The next significant evolution in money came with the development of paper money. The Chinese were the first to use paper currency during the Tang Dynasty (618–907 CE). By the Song Dynasty (960–1279 CE), paper money became widespread.

Paper money had several advantages over coins:

- Portability: Paper notes were lighter and easier to carry than metal coins.

- Efficiency: Printing money was cheaper and quicker than minting coins.

- Expansion of Trade: The use of paper money facilitated long-distance trade and the growth of economies.

The Gold Standard

By the 19th century, many countries adopted the gold standard, a system in which the value of currency was directly linked to gold. Under this system, countries agreed to convert paper money into a fixed amount of gold upon request.

The gold standard provided several benefits:

- Stability: It created a stable exchange rate system, promoting international trade.

- Trust: Linking currency to gold increased confidence in the monetary system.

- Inflation Control: It limited the amount of money that could be printed, helping control inflation.

However, the gold standard also had drawbacks:

- Limited Supply: The money supply was restricted by the amount of gold available.

- Economic Rigidity: It could lead to deflation and economic downturns during periods of gold scarcity.

The Rise of Fiat Money

The 20th century saw the transition from the gold standard to fiat money—currency that has value because a government decrees it so, rather than being backed by a physical commodity like gold.

Fiat money offered several advantages:

- Flexibility: Governments could adjust the money supply to respond to economic conditions.

- Economic Growth: It supported more dynamic and flexible economic policies.

- Reduced Dependence on Gold: Economies were no longer constrained by gold reserves.

However, fiat money also posed challenges:

- Inflation Risk: Without the discipline of the gold standard, there was a higher risk of inflation.

- Trust Issues: Fiat money relies heavily on public confidence in the issuing government.

The Digital Revolution

The late 20th and early 21st centuries brought about a digital revolution in money. Electronic banking, credit cards, and online payment systems transformed how people use and think about money. Key developments include:

- Electronic Funds Transfer (EFT): Enabled instant transfer of funds between accounts.

- Credit and Debit Cards: Provided convenience and security for everyday transactions.

- Online Banking: Allowed customers to manage their finances remotely.

The Emergence of Cryptocurrencies

The latest evolution in money is the advent of cryptocurrencies, digital or virtual currencies that use cryptography for security. Bitcoin, introduced in 2009, was the first decentralized cryptocurrency, and since then, thousands of cryptocurrencies have emerged.

Cryptocurrencies offer several potential benefits:

- Decentralization: Operate independently of central banks and governments.

- Security: Use blockchain technology to provide secure and transparent transactions.

- Innovation: Enable new forms of financial services and applications.

However, cryptocurrencies also face significant challenges:

- Volatility: Cryptocurrencies are often highly volatile, which can deter widespread adoption.

- Regulation: Governments are still grappling with how to regulate cryptocurrencies.

- Trust and Adoption: Widespread acceptance and trust are still in development.

Conclusion

The history and evolution of money demonstrate its profound impact on human behavior and societal structures. From the limitations of the barter system to the flexibility of fiat money and the innovation of cryptocurrencies, each transformation has influenced how people perceive, use, and manage money. Understanding this history is essential for grasping the psychological aspects of financial behavior and the ongoing evolution of the global economy.

This journey of money highlights the dynamic interplay between technological advancements, economic needs, and human psychology. As we move forward, the continuous evolution of money will undoubtedly shape future financial behaviors and societal norms in ways we can only begin to imagine.

CHAPTER 03

THE BASIS OF FINANCIAL PSYCHOLOGY

Financial psychology is an interdisciplinary field that merges insights from psychology and economics to explore how people make financial decisions. By understanding the cognitive, emotional, and social factors that influence financial behavior, financial psychology aims to provide a comprehensive view of why individuals act the way they do with money. This chapter introduces key concepts and theories in financial psychology, laying the foundation for a deeper exploration of this intriguing subject.

Key Concepts in Financial Psychology

1. Behavioral Economics

Behavioral economics is a subfield that combines psychological insights with economic theory to understand why people sometimes make irrational financial decisions. Unlike traditional economics, which assumes that individuals are rational actors always seeking to maximize utility, behavioral economics acknowledges that cognitive biases and emotions can lead to suboptimal decisions.

2. Cognitive Biases

Cognitive biases are systematic patterns of deviation from rationality in judgment, which can significantly impact financial decisions. Some common cognitive biases include:

- Overconfidence: The tendency to overestimate one's abilities or knowledge, leading to risky financial behaviors such as excessive trading or underestimating risks.

- Anchoring: The reliance on the first piece of information encountered (the "anchor") when making decisions, which can lead to inappropriate financial judgments.

- Loss Aversion: The tendency to prefer avoiding losses rather than acquiring equivalent gains, leading to conservative investment strategies or irrational decisions to hold onto losing assets.

3. Emotional Factors

Emotions play a crucial role in financial behavior. Feelings such as fear, greed, joy, and regret can drive financial actions and influence market trends. For example, fear can lead to panic selling during market downturns, while greed can drive speculative buying during market booms.

4. Social and Cultural Influences

Social and cultural factors also significantly shape financial behavior. These influences include family background, societal norms, and cultural values. For instance, people from different cultural backgrounds may have varying attitudes toward saving, spending, and investing.

Theories in Financial Psychology

1. Prospect Theory

Prospect theory, developed by Daniel Kahneman and Amos Tversky, is a cornerstone of behavioral economics. It describes how people make decisions under risk and uncertainty. Key insights from prospect theory include:

- Value Function: People evaluate potential losses and gains relative to a reference point rather than in absolute terms. This leads to loss aversion, where losses are felt more intensely than equivalent gains.

- Probability Weighting: People tend to overestimate the likelihood of low-probability events and underestimate the likelihood of high-probability events, which can lead to skewed risk perceptions.

2. Mental Accounting

Mental accounting, introduced by Richard Thaler, refers to the cognitive process by which individuals categorize and evaluate economic outcomes. People tend to assign money to different "accounts" based on its source or intended use, which can lead to irrational financial behaviors. For example, someone might treat a tax refund as "extra" money to spend frivolously, even though it is part of their overall income.

3. Self-control and Delayed Gratification

Self-control is a critical aspect of financial behavior. The ability to delay gratification—to forgo immediate rewards in favor of larger future benefits—is essential for saving and investing. The famous "marshmallow test" conducted by Walter Mischel demonstrated that children who could delay gratification were more likely to achieve better life outcomes, including financial success.

4. Herd Behavior

Herd behavior describes how individuals tend to follow the actions of a larger group, often ignoring their own judgment. In financial markets, herd behavior can lead to bubbles and crashes as people collectively drive prices up or down based on the actions of others rather than fundamental values.

Practical Applications of Financial Psychology

1. Financial Planning and Advising

Financial advisors can use insights from financial psychology to better understand their clients' behaviors and biases. By recognizing cognitive biases and emotional influences, advisors can tailor their advice to help clients make more rational financial decisions.

2. Behavioral Finance Interventions

Behavioral finance interventions aim to improve financial decision-making by addressing cognitive and emotional biases. Techniques such as "nudging" can encourage better financial behaviors without restricting freedom of choice. For example, automatically enrolling employees in retirement savings plans can increase participation rates.

3. Financial Education

Improving financial literacy is essential for helping individuals make informed financial decisions. Financial education programs that incorporate principles from financial psychology can more effectively teach people how to recognize and manage their biases and emotions in financial contexts.

4. Policy Making

Policymakers can use insights from financial psychology to design regulations and policies that promote better financial behaviors. For instance, regulations requiring clear and simple disclosures can help consumers make more informed choices about financial products.

Conclusion

Financial psychology provides a rich and nuanced understanding of the factors that influence financial behavior. By integrating insights from psychology and economics, this field offers valuable tools for improving financial decision-making at both individual and societal levels. As we continue to explore the complexities of financial behavior, the principles of financial psychology will play an increasingly important role in helping people achieve greater financial well-being.

CHAPTER 04

MONEY AND HUMAN BEHAVIOR

Money is a central component of modern life, influencing nearly every aspect of human behavior. From individual decisions to societal norms, the presence of money shapes how people think, feel, and act. This chapter provides an overview of the ways in which money affects human behavior, exploring the psychological mechanisms behind financial actions and their broader implications for relationships and society.

Money and Individual Behavior

1. Decision Making

Money significantly impacts individual decision-making processes. The availability or scarcity of money can alter choices in areas such as career, education, health, and lifestyle. Key aspects include:

- Risk Tolerance: Financial stability often influences an individual's willingness to take risks. Those with greater financial security may be more inclined to invest or pursue entrepreneurial ventures, while those with limited resources might adopt more conservative approaches.

- Value Perception: The subjective value assigned to money can affect decisions. For instance, people might perceive $100 as more valuable when it comes as a gift compared to earned income, influencing how they choose to spend or save it.

2. Emotional Responses

Money elicits strong emotional responses, which can drive behavior. Common emotions associated with money include:

- Joy and Satisfaction: Earning or receiving money often brings pleasure and a sense of accomplishment, which can motivate further financial pursuits.

- Stress and Anxiety: Financial pressures, such as debt or insufficient savings, can lead to significant stress and anxiety, affecting mental health and decision-making capabilities.

3. Self-identity and Esteem

Money plays a crucial role in shaping self-identity and self-esteem. The amount of money one has can influence their sense of worth and social status. Key points include:

- Status Symbols: Possessions and lifestyle choices funded by money can serve as symbols of success and status, impacting self-esteem and social interactions.

- Personal Fulfillment: For some, financial success is closely tied to personal fulfillment and life satisfaction, while for others, the pursuit of money can lead to an unending cycle of dissatisfaction.

Money and Relationships

1. Interpersonal Dynamics

Money can affect relationships in numerous ways, influencing dynamics between partners, family members, and friends. Key aspects include:

- Power and Control: In relationships, the person who controls the finances may hold more power, potentially leading to imbalances and conflicts.

- Trust and Transparency: Financial transparency is crucial for trust in relationships. Hidden debts or undisclosed spending can lead to significant issues.

2. Family and Upbringing

The financial behaviors learned in childhood often carry into adulthood. Families play a significant role in shaping attitudes toward money, including:

- Financial Education: Parents who teach their children about money management can instill positive financial habits.

- Inherited Behaviors: Children may adopt their parents' financial behaviors, whether frugal or spendthrift, which can influence their own financial success or struggles.

3. Social Influence

Social circles and peer pressure can significantly impact financial behavior. Keeping up with friends or societal expectations can drive spending habits, often leading to financial strain. Key points include:

- Conspicuous Consumption: The desire to display wealth through material possessions can lead to overspending and debt.

- Social Comparison: Constantly comparing oneself to others financially can lead to dissatisfaction and poor financial decisions.

Money and Societal Norms

1. Cultural Values

Cultural attitudes toward money vary widely and influence financial behavior. Different cultures have distinct views on spending, saving, and investing. For instance:

- Collectivist vs. Individualist Societies: Collectivist cultures may emphasize communal financial support and sharing resources, while individualist cultures may prioritize personal financial independence and wealth accumulation.

- Attitudes Toward Debt: Cultural norms influence attitudes toward borrowing and debt. Some cultures view debt as shameful, while others see it as a normal part of financial management.

2. Economic Systems

The structure of a society's economic system can shape financial behavior. Capitalist economies, for instance, may encourage entrepreneurial risk-taking and consumerism, while socialist economies might emphasize collective welfare and financial equality. Key aspects include:

- Income Inequality: High levels of income inequality can lead to social stratification and influence financial behaviors across different socioeconomic groups.

- Access to Financial Services: The availability of financial services, such as banking and credit, impacts how individuals manage their money.

3. Media and Advertising

Media and advertising play significant roles in shaping financial behavior by influencing desires and spending habits. Key points include:

- Consumer Culture: Media often promotes a consumer culture that encourages spending and materialism, impacting financial priorities.

- Financial Education: Media can also serve as a platform for financial education, providing information and tools to improve financial literacy.

The Broader Implications

1. Economic Behavior

The collective financial behaviors of individuals influence broader economic trends. For instance, high levels of consumer spending can drive economic growth, while widespread financial conservatism can lead to stagnation. Key points include:

- Market Dynamics: Individual investment decisions impact stock markets and financial markets, influencing economic stability and growth.

- Savings Rates: The aggregate savings behavior of a population affects national savings rates and economic policies.

2. Public Policy

Understanding the psychological mechanisms behind financial behavior can inform public policy. Policymakers can design interventions to promote better financial outcomes, such as:

- Financial Literacy Programs: Initiatives aimed at improving financial literacy can help individuals make informed decisions and improve their financial well-being.
- Regulations: Policies that protect consumers from predatory financial practices and provide safety nets can enhance financial stability and reduce economic disparities.

Conclusion

Money influences human behavior in multifaceted ways, affecting individual decisions, relationships, and societal norms. By understanding the psychological mechanisms behind financial behaviors, we can better navigate the complexities of money and its impact on our lives. This chapter provides an overview of the intricate relationship between money and human behavior, setting the stage for a deeper exploration of the psychological factors that drive financial actions. As we continue to examine these dynamics, we can develop more effective strategies for achieving financial well-being and fostering healthier economic environments.

CHAPTER 05

THE COGNITIVE BIASES AFFECTING FINANCIAL DECISIONS

Cognitive biases are systematic patterns of deviation from norm or rationality in judgment, which affect how people perceive and process information. These biases can lead to errors in thinking and decision-making, often resulting in suboptimal financial outcomes. Understanding these biases is crucial for making more informed and rational financial decisions. This chapter discusses some of the most common cognitive biases—overconfidence, loss aversion, anchoring, and others—and examines how they impact financial behavior.

Overconfidence

Overconfidence is the tendency to overestimate one's abilities, knowledge, and judgment. In the context of financial decisions, overconfidence can manifest in several ways:

1. Excessive Trading

Overconfident investors often engage in excessive trading, believing they can predict market movements better than they actually can. This can lead to higher transaction costs and poorer investment returns.

2. Underestimation of Risk

Overconfident individuals may underestimate the risks associated with their financial decisions, leading them to take on more risk than is prudent. This can result in significant financial losses, particularly in volatile markets.

3. Illusion of Control

Overconfidence can create an illusion of control, where individuals believe they have more influence over financial outcomes than they actually do. This can lead to poor decision-making and a failure to adequately prepare for adverse events.

Loss Aversion

Loss aversion refers to the tendency to prefer avoiding losses rather than acquiring equivalent gains. People feel the pain of losing money more acutely than the pleasure of gaining the same amount. This bias impacts financial decisions in several ways:

1. Holding on to Losing Investments

Investors often hold on to losing investments longer than they should, hoping to break even. This behavior, driven by loss aversion, can result in greater losses over time.

2. Conservative Investment Strategies

Loss aversion can lead individuals to adopt overly conservative investment strategies, avoiding higher-risk opportunities that could offer better returns. This can limit potential gains and hinder long-term financial growth.

3. Emotional Reactions

The fear of losses can trigger strong emotional reactions, such as panic selling during market downturns. These emotional responses can lead to poor timing in buying and selling investments, exacerbating financial losses.

Anchoring

Anchoring is the cognitive bias where individuals rely too heavily on the first piece of information they encounter (the "anchor") when making decisions. In financial contexts, anchoring can lead to several issues:

1. Price Anchoring

Investors may anchor on the purchase price of an investment, using it as a reference point for decisions. This can result in holding onto investments that have declined in value, rather than reassessing their potential based on current market conditions.

2. Forecasting and Projections

Anchoring can affect financial forecasting and projections. For example, an investor might base future expectations on past performance, ignoring changes in market conditions or new information that could impact outcomes.

3. Negotiations

In financial negotiations, the initial offer can serve as an anchor, influencing subsequent counteroffers and final agreements. This can lead to suboptimal outcomes if the initial anchor is not based on a realistic assessment of value.

Confirmation Bias

Confirmation bias is the tendency to search for, interpret, and remember information that confirms one's preexisting beliefs or hypotheses. This bias can significantly impact financial decisions:

1. Selective Information Gathering

Investors may seek out information that supports their investment decisions while ignoring or downplaying contradictory evidence. This can lead to overconfidence and poor decision-making.

2. Reinforcement of Poor Decisions

Once a financial decision is made, confirmation bias can lead individuals to continue supporting it despite evidence that it was a mistake. This can result in continued investment in losing assets or adherence to flawed strategies.

Hindsight Bias

Hindsight bias is the inclination to see events as having been predictable after they have already occurred. In financial contexts, this bias can affect behavior in several ways:

1. Overestimating Predictability

Investors may believe they "knew it all along" when a market event occurs, leading to overconfidence in their predictive abilities. This can result in increased risk-taking and subsequent losses.

2. Criticism of Past Decisions

Hindsight bias can lead individuals to harshly judge their past financial decisions, believing they should have seen the outcome coming. This can erode confidence and impact future decision-making.

Availability Heuristic

The availability heuristic is a mental shortcut that relies on immediate examples that come to mind when evaluating a topic or decision. This bias can skew financial decisions by:

1. Overemphasis on Recent Events

Recent market trends or financial news may disproportionately influence decisions, even if they are not indicative of long-term patterns. This can lead to reactive and short-sighted financial behavior.

2. Ignoring Statistical Probabilities

The availability heuristic can cause individuals to overestimate the likelihood of dramatic but rare events (e.g., market crashes) and underestimate the probability of more common, less newsworthy occurrences. This can result in misallocation of resources and inappropriate risk management.

Herd Behavior

Herd behavior describes the tendency for individuals to mimic the actions of a larger group, often disregarding their own analysis or intuition. In financial markets, herd behavior can lead to:

1. Market Bubbles

When investors collectively drive up the price of an asset beyond its intrinsic value, a market bubble forms. Herd behavior can exacerbate this phenomenon, leading to unsustainable price increases and eventual crashes.

2. Panic Selling

Conversely, herd behavior can also contribute to panic selling during market downturns, as individuals rush to sell off assets in response to others' actions. This can amplify market volatility and deepen losses.

Status Quo Bias

Status quo bias is the preference for maintaining the current state of affairs, even when change could be beneficial. In financial decision-making, this bias can manifest as:

1. Reluctance to Switch Investments

Investors may stick with underperforming investments due to the perceived effort or risk associated with change. This can lead to missed opportunities and suboptimal portfolio performance.

2. Resistance to Financial Planning

Individuals may avoid creating or updating financial plans, preferring to maintain their current approach despite potential benefits from proactive planning and adjustments.

Mitigating Cognitive Biases

Understanding and mitigating cognitive biases can lead to better financial decisions. Strategies include:

1. Awareness and Education

Recognizing common cognitive biases is the first step in mitigating their impact. Education on behavioral finance can help individuals identify and counteract biased thinking.

2. Objective Decision-Making

Using objective criteria and systematic approaches can reduce the influence of biases. For example, following a disciplined investment strategy based on fundamental analysis rather than emotions can lead to more rational decisions.

3. Seeking Diverse Perspectives

Consulting with financial advisors or peers can provide alternative viewpoints and reduce the risk of biased decision-making. Diverse perspectives can help identify blind spots and encourage more balanced assessments.

4. Regular Review and Reflection

Regularly reviewing financial decisions and outcomes can help individuals recognize patterns of biased behavior and make necessary adjustments. Reflecting on past decisions with a critical eye can promote continuous improvement.

Conclusion

Cognitive biases are pervasive and can significantly impact financial decision-making. By understanding these biases and implementing strategies to mitigate their effects, individuals can make more informed and rational financial choices. This chapter has highlighted some of the most common cognitive biases affecting financial behavior and provided insights into how they can be managed. As we continue to explore the psychology of money, recognizing and addressing cognitive biases will be crucial for achieving better financial outcomes and fostering a more rational approach to personal finance.

CHAPTER 06

NATURE'S WRATH

Emotions play a crucial role in financial decision-making. Fear, greed, joy, and regret can drive financial actions, often leading to irrational behaviors that deviate from logical economic models. This chapter examines how various emotions influence spending, saving, and investing behaviors, and discusses strategies to manage these emotional influences for better financial outcomes.

Fear

Fear is a powerful emotion that can significantly impact financial decisions. It often manifests in response to perceived threats or uncertainties, influencing behavior in several ways:

1. Panic Selling

During market downturns, fear can lead to panic selling, where investors rush to liquidate assets to avoid further losses. This behavior can exacerbate market declines and result in substantial financial losses for those who sell at the bottom.

2. Avoidance of Risk

Fear can make individuals overly cautious, leading them to avoid investments perceived as risky. While this can protect against losses, it can also result in missed opportunities for growth. For example, fear of stock market volatility might lead someone to keep their savings in low-yield accounts, sacrificing potential returns.

3. Emergency Savings

On a positive note, fear of financial instability can motivate individuals to build and maintain emergency savings. This precautionary behavior can provide a safety net in times of unexpected expenses or economic downturns.

Greed

Greed, or the excessive desire for wealth, can drive individuals to take undue risks in pursuit of higher returns. This emotion influences financial behavior in various ways:

1. Speculative Investments

Greed often leads to speculative investments in high-risk assets, such as cryptocurrencies or unproven startups. While these investments can offer substantial rewards, they also carry significant risks, which can lead to severe losses.

2. Overleveraging

In the pursuit of higher returns, individuals driven by greed may take on excessive debt to invest more than they can afford. Overleveraging can lead to financial ruin if the investments do not perform as expected, leaving the individual unable to repay their debts.

3. Chasing Trends

Greed can cause investors to chase market trends, buying into assets that have recently performed well without considering their long-term viability. This behavior can result in buying high and selling low, leading to financial losses.

Joy

Joy, or positive emotional experiences, can also influence financial behavior. While it often leads to increased spending, it can also promote generous and proactive financial actions:

1. Impulse Spending

Experiencing joy or excitement can lead to impulse spending, where individuals make spontaneous purchases driven by positive emotions. While this can result in temporary happiness, it can also lead to financial strain if not managed carefully.

2. Generosity

Positive emotions can encourage generosity, leading individuals to donate to charities, support friends or family, or invest in causes they care about. While these actions can be financially positive, they should be balanced with personal financial stability.

3. Proactive Financial Planning

Joy and contentment with one's financial situation can promote proactive financial planning. Individuals who feel positive about their finances are more likely to engage in budgeting, saving, and investing for future goals.

Regret

Regret is a powerful emotion that can have a profound impact on financial decisions. It often arises from missed opportunities or poor financial choices, influencing behavior in several ways:

1. Risk Aversion

Fear of future regret can lead to risk-averse behavior, where individuals avoid making financial decisions altogether. This can result in missed opportunities for growth and financial improvement.

2. Revising Financial Strategies

Experiencing regret from past financial mistakes can motivate individuals to revise their financial strategies and seek better advice. Learning from past errors can lead to more informed and cautious decision-making in the future.

3. Overcompensation

Regret can also lead to overcompensation, where individuals swing to the opposite extreme in an attempt to rectify past mistakes. For example, someone who regrets not investing earlier may become overly aggressive in their investment strategy, taking on too much risk.

Managing Emotional Influences

Recognizing and managing emotional influences is crucial for making sound financial decisions. Here are some strategies to help:

. Emotional Awareness

Being aware of one's emotional state and understanding how it influences decision-making is the first step toward managing emotions. Mindfulness practices and reflective thinking can help individuals recognize when emotions are driving their financial behavior.

2. Establishing Rules and Plans

Setting clear financial rules and plans can help mitigate the impact of emotions. For example, having a predetermined investment strategy or spending plan can provide a framework that reduces the likelihood of impulsive decisions driven by fear or greed.

3. Seeking Professional Advice

Financial advisors can provide an objective perspective, helping individuals make decisions based on rational analysis rather than emotional reactions. Regular consultations with a financial advisor can help keep emotional influences in check.

4. Diversification and Risk Management

Diversifying investments and employing risk management strategies can reduce the emotional impact of market fluctuations. Knowing that one's portfolio is well-balanced can provide peace of mind and reduce fear-driven decisions.

5. Building Financial Literacy

Increasing financial literacy can empower individuals to make informed decisions, reducing the influence of emotions. Understanding financial concepts and market dynamics can provide confidence and reduce anxiety related to financial choices.

Conclusion

Emotions play a critical role in financial behavior, influencing decisions in complex and often subconscious ways. By understanding the emotional factors that drive financial actions, individuals can develop strategies to manage these influences and make more rational, informed decisions.

This chapter has explored the roles of fear, greed, joy, and regret in financial behavior, highlighting the importance of emotional awareness and management in achieving financial well-being. As we continue to examine the psychology of money, recognizing and addressing emotional influences will be essential for fostering healthier financial habits and outcomes.

CHAPTER 07

BEHAVIOR ECONOMICS AND ITS IMPACT ON FINANCE

Behavioral economics is a field that bridges the gap between psychology and economics, challenging the traditional assumption that individuals always make rational decisions aimed at maximizing utility. By incorporating psychological insights into economic theory, behavioral economics provides a more nuanced understanding of financial behavior. This chapter explores key concepts from behavioral economics, such as "nudging," and examines their implications for financial behavior and policy.

The Foundations of Behavioral Economics

Behavioral economics emerged as a response to the limitations of classical economic theories that assume rational behavior. Key figures like Daniel Kahneman, Amos Tversky, and Richard Thaler have contributed significantly to this field, highlighting how cognitive biases, emotions, and social factors influence economic decisions.

1. Prospect Theory

Developed by Daniel Kahneman and Amos Tversky, prospect theory is foundational in behavioral economics. It describes how people make decisions under risk and uncertainty, emphasizing two main components:

- Value Function: People evaluate potential losses and gains relative to a reference point rather than in absolute terms. Losses typically have a greater emotional impact than equivalent gains, a phenomenon known as loss aversion.
- Probability Weighting: People tend to overestimate the likelihood of unlikely events and underestimate the likelihood of likely events, leading to skewed perceptions of risk.

2. Mental Accounting

Richard Thaler introduced the concept of mental accounting, which refers to the cognitive process by which individuals categorize and evaluate financial activities. People often assign money to different "accounts" based on subjective criteria, which can lead to irrational financial behaviors. For example, someone might treat a tax refund as "extra" money to spend freely, even though it is part of their overall income.

3. Bounded Rationality

Herbert Simon's concept of bounded rationality acknowledges that individuals have limited cognitive resources, time, and information. Consequently, they use heuristics or rules of thumb to make decisions rather than conducting exhaustive analyses. This often results in satisfactory rather than optimal outcomes.

Key Concepts in Behavioral Economics

1. Nudging

Nudging involves subtly guiding individuals toward better decisions without restricting their freedom of choice. Richard Thaler and Cass Sunstein popularized this concept in their book "Nudge," highlighting how small changes in the environment can significantly influence behavior. Examples of nudges include:

- Default Options: Setting beneficial options as defaults, such as automatic enrollment in retirement savings plans, can increase participation rates.
- Framing Effects: Presenting information in different ways can impact decisions. For example, highlighting the benefits of saving versus the costs of not saving can encourage better financial behavior.

2. Hyperbolic Discounting

Hyperbolic discounting describes the tendency for people to prefer smaller, immediate rewards over larger, delayed rewards. This bias can lead to impulsive financial decisions, such as overspending and inadequate saving for the future. Recognizing this bias can help in designing interventions that encourage long-term financial planning.

3. Status Quo Bias

Status quo bias is the preference for maintaining the current state of affairs, even when change could be beneficial. This bias can result in inertia in financial behavior, such as sticking with default investment options or failing to update financial plans. Understanding status quo bias can help in creating strategies to prompt proactive financial decisions.

4. Endowment Effect

The endowment effect is the tendency for people to value something more highly simply because they own it. This bias can impact financial decisions, such as holding onto underperforming assets or overvaluing personal possessions. Awareness of the endowment effect can lead to more objective financial evaluations.

Implications for Financial Behavior

1. Investment Decisions

Behavioral economics provides valuable insights into how biases affect investment decisions. Understanding these biases can help investors make more rational choices:

- Diversification: Recognizing the tendency to overinvest in familiar assets (home bias) can encourage diversification to reduce risk.

- Market Timing: Awareness of overconfidence and herding behavior can help investors avoid the pitfalls of market timing and speculative bubbles.

2. Saving and Spending

Behavioral economics highlights the psychological factors that influence saving and spending behaviors. Practical applications include:

- Automatic Enrollment: Setting up automatic transfers to savings accounts can help overcome procrastination and inertia.

- Commitment Devices: Using tools that restrict access to savings or impose penalties for early withdrawal can help individuals adhere to long-term financial goals.

3. Debt Management

Understanding behavioral biases can improve debt management strategies. Key insights include:

- Debt Aversion: Framing debt repayment in a way that highlights progress can motivate individuals to pay off debts more aggressively.

- Minimum Payments: Highlighting the long-term costs of making only minimum payments on credit cards can encourage higher repayments and faster debt reduction.

Implications for Public Policy

1. Financial Literacy Programs

Behavioral economics underscores the importance of financial literacy in improving financial behavior. Policymakers can design educational programs that:

- Simplify Complex Concepts: Use clear, relatable examples to explain financial principles.

- Behavioral Interventions: Incorporate nudges and commitment devices to reinforce positive financial behaviors.

2. Consumer Protection

Behavioral insights can inform consumer protection regulations to prevent exploitation by financial institutions. Examples include:

- Transparent Disclosures: Mandating clear and simple disclosures for financial products can help consumers make informed decisions.

- Regulating Predatory Practices: Implementing rules to protect consumers from high-cost loans and deceptive marketing practices.

3. Retirement Planning

Policymakers can use behavioral economics to design retirement planning initiatives that encourage long-term saving. Strategies include:

- Automatic Enrollment and Escalation: Automatically enrolling employees in retirement plans and gradually increasing contribution rates can significantly boost retirement savings.

- Incentive Structures: Providing matching contributions or tax incentives can further encourage participation in retirement plans.

The Future of Behavioral Economics in Finance

Behavioral economics continues to evolve, offering new insights and applications for improving financial behavior. Emerging trends include:

- Digital Nudges: Using technology to deliver personalized nudges based on individual financial behavior.

- Behavioral Data Analytics: Analyzing large datasets to identify patterns and develop targeted interventions for improving financial decision-making.

- Global Applications: Adapting behavioral economics principles to different cultural and economic contexts to address unique financial challenges.

Conclusion

Behavioral economics offers a rich framework for understanding and improving financial behavior by integrating psychological insights into economic decision-making. By recognizing and addressing cognitive biases, emotions, and social influences, individuals and policymakers can make more informed and rational financial decisions. This chapter has explored key concepts from behavioral economics, such as nudging, hyperbolic discounting, and status quo bias, and examined their implications for personal finance and public policy. As the field continues to develop, it will provide even more tools and strategies for enhancing financial well-being and economic stability.

CHAPTER 08

THE INFLUENCE OF SOCIAL AND CULTURAL FACTORS

Social and cultural factors play a critical role in shaping financial behavior. These influences encompass family background, societal norms, and cultural values, all of which contribute to how individuals perceive and manage money. This chapter investigates how these factors shape financial attitudes and practices, providing a comprehensive understanding of the social and cultural dimensions of financial behavior.

Family Background

1. Parental Influence

Parents are often the first source of financial education for children. The financial habits and attitudes exhibited by parents can significantly influence their children's future financial behavior. Key aspects include:

- Financial Literacy: Parents who discuss money management and involve their children in financial decisions can instill good financial habits early on.

- Modeling Behavior: Children often emulate their parents' financial behaviors, whether they are frugal, spendthrift, or somewhere in between.

- Financial Support: The level of financial support parents provide, such as allowances or contributions to education, can shape children's attitudes toward earning and saving money.

2. Socioeconomic Status

The socioeconomic status (SES) of a family can impact financial behavior in several ways:

- Access to Resources: Families with higher SES often have better access to financial education, investment opportunities, and financial planning resources.

- Financial Stability: Lower SES families may face financial instability, influencing their attitudes toward saving and risk-taking.

- Expectations and Aspirations: SES can shape financial aspirations and expectations, with higher SES families often setting higher financial goals for their children.

3. Intergenerational Wealth Transfer

The transfer of wealth and financial knowledge across generations can significantly impact financial behavior. Key points include:

- Inheritance: Receiving an inheritance can provide financial stability and opportunities for investment, shaping future financial decisions.

- Financial Education: Passing down financial knowledge and best practices can equip younger generations with the tools to manage money effectively.

Societal Norms

1. Consumer Culture

Societal norms around consumption and materialism can strongly influence financial behavior. Consumer culture often promotes the acquisition of goods and services as a pathway to happiness and status. Key aspects include:

- Advertising and Media: Constant exposure to advertising and media can create desires for new products and lifestyles, driving spending behavior.

- Social Comparison: Comparing oneself to others, often through social media, can lead to pressure to spend and keep up with peers.

2. Saving and Investment Norms

Different societies have varying norms around saving and investing. These norms can influence how individuals approach financial planning. Examples include:

- Saving Rates: Societies that emphasize frugality and long-term planning tend to have higher saving rates. For instance, many East Asian cultures prioritize saving over spending.
- Investment Preferences: Cultural attitudes can shape preferences for certain types of investments, such as real estate versus stocks.

3. Debt Attitudes

Cultural norms around debt can influence financial behavior significantly. Key points include:

- Acceptance of Debt: In some cultures, taking on debt is a common practice for funding education, home purchases, or starting businesses. In others, debt is viewed negatively, and individuals may avoid borrowing even for beneficial purposes.
- Debt Management: Cultural attitudes toward debt repayment and management can impact financial behavior. For example, in some cultures, repaying debt promptly is a matter of personal honor.

Cultural Values

1. Collectivism vs. Individualism

Cultural values around collectivism and individualism can shape financial behavior in distinct ways:

- Collectivist Cultures: In collectivist societies, financial decisions are often made with the well-being of the family or community in mind. This can lead to more communal financial practices, such as pooling resources or supporting extended family members.

- Individualist Cultures: In individualist cultures, financial decisions tend to prioritize personal goals and independence. This can lead to more individualistic financial behaviors, such as personal savings and investments.

2. Religious and Ethical Beliefs

Religious and ethical beliefs can influence financial behavior by providing moral guidelines for money management. Examples include:

- Charitable Giving: Many religions encourage or mandate charitable giving, influencing how individuals allocate their financial resources.

- Ethical Investments: Religious or ethical beliefs may guide investment choices, such as avoiding investments in certain industries or seeking socially responsible investments.

3. Work Ethic and Achievement

Cultural values around work ethic and achievement can impact financial behavior:

- Hard Work and Success: Cultures that emphasize hard work and success may drive individuals to pursue higher education, career advancement, and entrepreneurial endeavors, influencing their financial behaviors and goals.
- Attitudes Toward Leisure: Cultural values around leisure and consumption can shape how individuals balance work and spending. For example, some cultures may prioritize saving for future leisure, while others may emphasize enjoying the present.

The Role of Education and Socialization

1. Financial Education

Formal and informal financial education plays a crucial role in shaping financial behavior. Key points include:

- School Programs: Financial literacy programs in schools can provide foundational knowledge about money management, saving, and investing.
- Community Initiatives: Community-based financial education initiatives can reach diverse populations, offering practical advice and resources for managing money.

2. Socialization Agents

Various socialization agents, such as peers, media, and institutions, influence financial behavior. Examples include:

- Peer Influence: Friends and peers can impact financial behavior through social interactions and shared experiences.

- Media and Technology: Exposure to financial news, social media influencers, and financial technology platforms can shape attitudes and behaviors related to money.

Global Perspectives

1. Cultural Differences in Financial Behavior

Different cultural contexts result in varying financial behaviors. Key examples include:

- Savings and Investment Practices: Comparing savings rates and investment behaviors across countries reveals cultural differences. For instance, countries like China and Japan have high savings rates, while countries like the United States have lower savings rates and higher consumer spending.

- Risk Tolerance: Cultural attitudes toward risk can influence investment strategies. For example, some cultures may be more conservative, favoring safe investments, while others may be more willing to take risks.

2. Migration and Financial Behavior

Migration can influence financial behavior by exposing individuals to new cultural norms and economic systems. Key points include:

- Adaptation to New Norms: Immigrants may adapt their financial behaviors to align with the norms of their new country, leading to changes in saving, spending, and investing practices.

- Remittances: Migrants often send money back to their home countries, impacting both their personal financial behavior and the economies of their home countries.

Implications for Financial Planning and Policy

1. Personal Financial Planning

Understanding the influence of social and cultural factors can enhance personal financial planning. Key strategies include:

- Tailoring Financial Plans: Financial advisors can tailor plans to consider clients' cultural values, family dynamics, and social influences.

- Cultural Competence: Financial professionals can benefit from cultural competence, understanding the diverse backgrounds and values of their clients to provide more effective advice.

2. Public Policy

Policymakers can design initiatives that account for social and cultural influences on financial behavior. Key considerations include:

- Inclusive Financial Education: Developing inclusive financial education programs that respect cultural differences and address diverse needs.

- Culturally Sensitive Policies: Creating policies that recognize and accommodate cultural values, such as supporting community-based financial practices or providing culturally relevant financial products.

Conclusion

Social and cultural factors significantly shape financial behavior, influencing how individuals perceive and manage money. By understanding the impact of family background, societal norms, and cultural values, we can gain deeper insights into financial attitudes and practices. This chapter has explored the various dimensions of social and cultural influences on financial behavior, highlighting their implications for personal financial planning and public policy. As we continue to examine the psychology of money, recognizing and addressing these social and cultural factors will be essential for fostering healthier financial behaviors and achieving greater financial well-being.

CHAPTER 09

WEALTH AND HAPPINESS: UNDERSTANDING THE CONNECTION

The age-old question, "Does money buy happiness?" has intrigued philosophers, economists, and psychologists for centuries. Understanding the complex relationship between wealth and well-being is crucial for grasping how financial status affects happiness and life satisfaction. This chapter delves into research findings and theoretical perspectives to explore how money influences happiness, the limits of this influence, and the factors that mediate the connection between wealth and well-being.

Theoretical Perspectives on Wealth and Happiness

1. Maslow's Hierarchy of Needs

Maslow's hierarchy of needs provides a framework for understanding the role of money in achieving happiness. According to this theory, human needs are arranged in a hierarchy, starting with basic physiological needs and progressing to safety, love and belonging, esteem, and self-actualization. Money primarily addresses the lower levels of the hierarchy:

- Physiological Needs: Money ensures access to basic necessities such as food, shelter, and healthcare.

- Safety Needs: Financial stability provides a sense of security and freedom from anxiety about future needs.

Once these basic needs are met, the incremental utility of money decreases, and other factors such as relationships, self-esteem, and personal fulfillment become more significant for happiness.

2. Easterlin Paradox

The Easterlin Paradox, named after economist Richard Easterlin, suggests that while wealthier individuals within a country tend to be happier than poorer individuals, increases in a country's average income do not correlate with increases in average happiness over time. This paradox highlights the relative nature of happiness and the importance of social comparisons.

3. Hedonic Treadmill

The hedonic treadmill theory posits that individuals quickly return to a baseline level of happiness following positive or negative life changes. As people become accustomed to higher levels of income or material wealth, their expectations and desires increase, leading to a continuous pursuit of more without a corresponding increase in long-term happiness.

Research Findings on Wealth and Happiness

1. Income and Happiness

Numerous studies have examined the relationship between income and happiness, revealing several key insights:

- Diminishing Returns: Research consistently shows that the correlation between income and happiness diminishes as income increases. While higher income boosts happiness at lower income levels by meeting basic needs and providing security, the additional happiness gained from further income increases is relatively small.

- Satiation Point: Studies suggest there is a satiation point beyond which additional income has negligible effects on happiness. For example, a study by Daniel Kahneman and Angus Deaton found that in the United States, the positive impact of income on emotional well-being plateaus at around $75,000 per year.

2. Wealth and Life Satisfaction

Wealth, encompassing assets and net worth in addition to income, also influences life satisfaction:

- Financial Security: Having substantial wealth provides a buffer against economic uncertainties, contributing to higher life satisfaction and lower stress levels.

- Freedom and Choices: Wealth affords greater freedom and a wider array of choices, enabling individuals to pursue activities and lifestyles that align with their values and interests.

3. Spending and Happiness

How individuals spend their money can significantly impact their happiness:

- Experiential Purchases: Research indicates that spending money on experiences, such as travel, concerts, and dining out, leads to greater and more lasting happiness than spending money on material goods. Experiences provide opportunities for social connection and create lasting memories.

- Prosocial Spending: Spending money on others, such as through gifts or charitable donations, is associated with higher levels of happiness compared to spending money on oneself. Prosocial spending fosters social connections and enhances one's sense of purpose and fulfillment.

Mediating Factors in the Wealth-Happiness Relationship

1. Social Comparisons

Social comparisons play a crucial role in how wealth affects happiness:

- Relative Wealth: Individuals often assess their financial well-being relative to others. Keeping up with peers or feeling wealthier than others can boost happiness while perceiving oneself as poorer can diminish it.

- Aspirational Gaps: The gap between one's current financial status and their financial aspirations can impact happiness. A large gap can lead to dissatisfaction while achieving or exceeding aspirations can enhance happiness.

2. Financial Management

Effective financial management can enhance the positive impact of wealth on happiness:

- Debt Management: High levels of debt, particularly high-interest debt such as credit card debt, can negate the positive effects of income and wealth on happiness. Managing and reducing debt is crucial for financial well-being.

- Savings and Investments: Having savings and investments can provide a sense of security and future-oriented satisfaction, contributing to overall happiness.

3. Personal Values and Priorities

Individual values and priorities mediate the relationship between wealth and happiness:

- Materialism: People who prioritize material wealth and possessions often report lower levels of happiness compared to those who value relationships, personal growth, and experiences.

- Purpose and Meaning: Individuals who use their wealth to pursue meaningful goals and contribute to causes they care about tend to experience higher levels of happiness.

Cultural and Societal Influences

1. Cultural Norms

Cultural norms and values influence how wealth affects happiness:

- Collectivist vs. Individualist Cultures: In collectivist cultures, financial success may be more closely tied to social responsibilities and communal well-being, while in individualist cultures, personal financial achievement may be more central to happiness.

- Cultural Attitudes Toward Wealth: Cultural attitudes toward wealth accumulation, consumption, and generosity can shape how financial status influences happiness.

2. Economic Inequality

Economic inequality within a society impacts the wealth-happiness relationship:

- Perceptions of Fairness: High levels of economic inequality can lead to perceptions of unfairness and social discontent, which can diminish overall happiness.

- Social Cohesion: Societies with lower levels of economic inequality tend to exhibit higher levels of social cohesion and trust, contributing to greater overall happiness.

Practical Implications for Enhancing Happiness

1. Focusing on Experiences

Prioritizing spending on experiences rather than material goods can enhance happiness. Experiences foster social connections, create lasting memories, and provide a sense of fulfillment.

2. Engaging in Prosocial Spending

Allocating resources to help others, whether through charitable donations or supporting loved ones, can boost happiness by enhancing social connections and a sense of purpose.

3. Managing Financial Stress

Effectively managing financial stress through budgeting, saving, and debt reduction can enhance the positive effects of wealth on happiness. Financial planning and seeking professional advice can provide strategies for achieving financial stability and reducing anxiety.

4. Aligning Wealth with Values

Using wealth to pursue personal values and meaningful goals can enhance happiness. This might include investing in education, supporting causes one cares about, or pursuing passions and hobbies that bring joy and fulfillment.

Conclusion

The relationship between wealth and happiness is complex and influenced by a multitude of factors. While money can contribute to happiness by meeting basic needs and providing security, its incremental value diminishes beyond a certain point. Social comparisons, effective financial management, and aligning financial resources with personal values are crucial for maximizing the positive impact of wealth on happiness. This chapter has explored the intricate connections between wealth and well-being, providing insights into how financial status affects life satisfaction and offering practical strategies for enhancing happiness through thoughtful financial decisions. Understanding these dynamics is essential for achieving a balanced and fulfilling life, where money serves as a tool for enhancing overall well-being rather than an end in itself.

CHAPTER 10

THE PSYCHOLOGY OF SPENDING

Spending money is more than a simple financial transaction; it is deeply intertwined with psychological factors that influence consumer behavior and spending patterns. Understanding the psychology behind spending can help individuals make more informed decisions and manage their finances better. This chapter explores the psychological triggers and motivations behind spending, examining how emotions, cognitive biases, social influences, and personal values shape consumer behavior.

Emotional Triggers

1. Retail Therapy

Many people engage in "retail therapy," where shopping is used as a way to improve mood and cope with negative emotions. The act of purchasing can provide a temporary boost in happiness and reduce feelings of stress, anxiety, or sadness. Key points include:

- Dopamine Release: The anticipation of buying something new triggers the release of dopamine, a neurotransmitter associated with pleasure and reward.
- Short-term Relief: While retail therapy can offer short-term emotional relief, it often leads to long-term financial stress if not managed properly.

2. Impulse Buying

Impulse buying refers to unplanned purchases driven by sudden urges. Emotional triggers such as excitement, boredom, or even sadness can lead to spontaneous spending. Factors that contribute to impulse buying include:

- Emotional States: People in heightened emotional states, whether positive or negative, are more likely to make impulsive purchases.
- Instant Gratification: The desire for immediate rewards can override long-term financial planning, leading to impulsive spending decisions.

Cognitive Biases

1. Anchoring

Anchoring occurs when individuals rely heavily on the first piece of information they encounter (the "anchor") when making decisions. In spending, anchoring can affect perceptions of value and price. Examples include:

- Sale Prices: Retailers often use original prices as anchors, making sale prices appear more attractive. Consumers may perceive a discount as a better deal than it actually is.

- Reference Points: Setting a high initial price for a product can make subsequent lower prices seem more reasonable, even if they are still relatively high.

2. Loss Aversion

Loss aversion is the tendency to prefer avoiding losses over acquiring equivalent gains. In spending, this can manifest in several ways:

- Reluctance to Return Items: Consumers may keep purchases they don't need or want because returning them feels like a loss.

- Sunk Cost Fallacy: People may continue spending on an activity or product they no longer value because they have already invested money in it.

3. Scarcity Effect

The scarcity effect refers to the perception that items are more valuable when they are scarce or limited in availability. This cognitive bias can drive spending behavior by creating a sense of urgency:

- Limited-Time Offers: Retailers use limited-time offers to create a fear of missing out (FOMO), prompting consumers to make quick purchasing decisions.

- Exclusive Products: Items marketed as rare or exclusive can attract higher demand and justify higher prices.

Social Influences

1. Social Proof

Social proof is the tendency to look to others for cues on how to behave. In spending, social proof can influence decisions in various ways:

- Reviews and Ratings: Positive reviews and high ratings can encourage consumers to purchase products they might otherwise hesitate to buy.

- Celebrity Endorsements: Endorsements from celebrities or influencers can significantly impact consumer choices by leveraging their perceived authority or popularity.

2. Peer Pressure

Peer pressure can lead individuals to conform to the spending habits of their social group. Key points include:

- Keeping Up with Peers: The desire to fit in or keep up with friends and peers can drive individuals to spend money on similar products or experiences.

- Social Comparison: Comparing oneself to others can lead to unnecessary spending to maintain a certain social status or image.

Personal Values and Identity

1. Self-Identity and Expression

Spending can be a way for individuals to express their self-identity and personal values. This includes:

- Lifestyle Choices: Consumers often purchase products that align with their lifestyle and personal values, such as eco-friendly products for environmentally conscious individuals.

- Brand Loyalty: Brand loyalty can reflect a consumer's identity and values. For example, someone might consistently buy products from a brand they perceive as innovative or socially responsible.

2. Emotional Connections to Brands

Brands can evoke strong emotional connections, influencing spending behavior. Factors contributing to brand loyalty include:

- Positive Experiences: Positive past experiences with a brand can lead to repeat purchases and a strong emotional attachment.

- Brand Narratives: Brands that tell compelling stories or align with a consumer's personal narrative can foster loyalty and drive spending.

Marketing and Advertising Techniques

1. Emotional Appeal

Marketers often use emotional appeals to connect with consumers on a deeper level. Techniques include:

- Storytelling: Ads that tell a story can create an emotional bond with the audience, making them more likely to purchase the product.
- Emotional Triggers: Advertisements that evoke emotions such as happiness, nostalgia, or empathy can drive consumer behavior.

2. Behavioral Targeting

Behavioral targeting involves using data on consumer behavior to deliver personalized advertisements. This technique can significantly influence spending patterns by:

- Personalized Recommendations: Offering tailored product recommendations based on past behavior can increase the likelihood of purchase.
- Retargeting: Ads that follow consumers across different platforms can remind them of products they viewed but did not purchase, encouraging them to complete the transaction.

Practical Strategies for Managing Spending

1. Budgeting

Creating and adhering to a budget is a fundamental strategy for managing spending. Key steps include:

- Tracking Expenses: Keeping track of all expenditures can help identify spending patterns and areas for potential savings.

- Setting Limits: Establishing spending limits for different categories can prevent overspending and ensure that essential expenses are covered.

2. Mindful Spending

Practicing mindful spending involves being aware of the motivations and consequences of spending decisions. Strategies include:

- Pause Before Purchasing: Taking a moment to reflect on whether a purchase is necessary and aligns with one's values can reduce impulse buying.

- Evaluating Needs vs. Wants: Differentiating between needs and wants can help prioritize essential spending and avoid unnecessary expenses.

3. Avoiding Temptation

Reducing exposure to spending triggers can help manage spending behavior. Tactics include:

- Unsubscribing from Marketing Emails: Reducing the number of promotional emails received can decrease the temptation to make unnecessary purchases.

- Limiting Social Media Use: Spending less time on social media can reduce exposure to influencer promotions and peer comparisons.

Conclusion

The psychology of spending is influenced by a myriad of factors, including emotions, cognitive biases, social influences, and personal values. By understanding these psychological triggers, individuals can develop strategies to manage their spending behavior more effectively. This chapter has explored the various motivations behind consumer behavior, highlighting the importance of mindful spending and financial management. As we continue to delve into the psychology of money, recognizing and addressing the psychological aspects of spending will be crucial for achieving greater financial well-being and making informed financial decisions.

CHAPTER 11

THE PSYCHOLOGY OF SAVING AND INVESTING

Saving and investing are crucial components of financial well-being, yet they are influenced by a complex interplay of psychological factors. Understanding the mindset and habits that contribute to effective saving and investing can help individuals achieve their financial goals. This chapter explores the psychological underpinnings of saving and investing behaviors, examining concepts such as delayed gratification, risk tolerance, and the cognitive biases that can impact financial decisions.

The Importance of Saving and Investing

Saving and investing serve different but complementary purposes in personal finance:

- Saving: Provides a safety net for emergencies, enables short-term goals, and offers liquidity.

- Investing: Helps grow wealth over the long term through the appreciation of assets, generating returns that outpace inflation.

Delayed Gratification

1. The Concept of Delayed Gratification

Delayed gratification is the ability to resist the temptation of an immediate reward in favor of a larger, more enduring reward in the future. This concept is foundational to effective saving and investing:

- Marshmallow Test: The famous "marshmallow test" conducted by Walter Mischel demonstrated that children who could delay gratification were more likely to achieve better life outcomes, including financial success.

2. Implications for Saving and Investing

Delayed gratification plays a significant role in financial behavior:

- Savings Accumulation: Individuals who can delay gratification are more likely to save money consistently, building a financial cushion for future needs.

- Long-term Investing: Delaying gratification allows investors to stay committed to long-term investment strategies, benefiting from compound growth over time.

3. Strategies to Enhance Delayed Gratification

Developing the ability to delay gratification can improve saving and investing habits:

- Goal Setting: Setting clear, achievable financial goals can provide motivation to save and invest rather than spending impulsively.
- Automatic Savings Plans: Automating savings contributions can help individuals prioritize saving without having to rely on willpower alone.
- Visualization: Visualizing future financial success can reinforce the benefits of delayed gratification, making it easier to resist immediate temptations.

Risk Tolerance

1. Understanding Risk Tolerance

Risk tolerance is the degree to which an individual is comfortable with the uncertainty and potential loss associated with investments. It varies based on personality, financial situation, and life stage:

- Risk Averse: Individuals who prefer stability and are uncomfortable with volatility.
- Risk Tolerant: Individuals who are willing to accept higher levels of risk for the potential of greater returns.

2. Factors Influencing Risk Tolerance

Several factors influence an individual's risk tolerance:

- Financial Situation: Those with a stable income and substantial savings may be more willing to take risks compared to those with limited financial resources.

- Personality Traits: Personality traits such as openness to experience and optimism can affect risk tolerance.

- Age and Life Stage: Younger individuals often have a higher risk tolerance due to a longer investment horizon, while older individuals nearing retirement may prefer safer investments.

3. Assessing and Managing Risk Tolerance

Understanding and managing risk tolerance is essential for successful investing:

- Risk Assessment Tools: Online questionnaires and financial advisor consultations can help individuals assess their risk tolerance.

- Diversification: Diversifying investments across asset classes can help manage risk by reducing the impact of any single investment's poor performance.

- Regular Reviews: Periodically reviewing and adjusting investment portfolios can ensure they remain aligned with changing risk tolerance and financial goals.

Cognitive Biases Affecting Saving and Investing

1. Overconfidence

Overconfidence is the tendency to overestimate one's knowledge and abilities. In investing, this can lead to excessive trading and taking unnecessary risks, often resulting in lower returns:

- Mitigation Strategies: Seeking professional advice and adhering to a disciplined investment strategy can help counteract overconfidence.

2. Loss Aversion

Loss aversion is the tendency to prefer avoiding losses over acquiring equivalent gains. This bias can lead to conservative investment strategies and reluctance to sell losing investments:

- Mitigation Strategies: Focusing on long-term goals and using systematic investment plans can help reduce the emotional impact of short-term losses.

3. Herd Behavior

Herd behavior occurs when individuals follow the actions of a larger group, often leading to buying high and selling low:

- Mitigation Strategies: Conducting independent research and maintaining a long-term perspective can help individuals avoid the pitfalls of herd behavior.

4. Mental Accounting

Mental accounting refers to the tendency to categorize and treat money differently based on its source or intended use. This can lead to suboptimal financial decisions, such as keeping savings in low-interest accounts while carrying high-interest debt:

- Mitigation Strategies: Viewing all assets and liabilities as part of a comprehensive financial picture can lead to more rational decision-making.

Habits for Effective Saving and Investing

1. Consistent Saving

Consistent saving habits are crucial for building wealth over time:

- Pay Yourself First: Prioritizing savings by automatically transferring a portion of income into savings or investment accounts before spending can ensure consistent contributions.
- Emergency Fund: Building and maintaining an emergency fund can provide financial security and prevent the need to dip into long-term investments for unexpected expenses.

2. Strategic Investing

Developing a strategic approach to investing can enhance long-term financial success:

- Asset Allocation: Diversifying investments across different asset classes (stocks, bonds, real estate) can balance risk and return.

- Rebalancing: Periodically rebalancing the portfolio to maintain the desired asset allocation can help manage risk and optimize returns.

- Dollar-Cost Averaging: Investing a fixed amount regularly, regardless of market conditions, can reduce the impact of market volatility and lower the average cost per share.

3. Continuous Learning

Staying informed about financial markets and investment strategies can improve decision-making:

- Financial Education: Continuously educating oneself about personal finance, investing, and market trends can build confidence and competence.

- Professional Advice: Seeking guidance from financial advisors or mentors can provide valuable insights and help avoid common pitfalls.

The Role of Financial Goals

1. Setting Clear Goals

Establishing clear financial goals provides direction and motivation for saving and investing:

- Short-term Goals: Goals such as building an emergency fund or saving for a vacation can provide immediate motivation.

- Long-term Goals: Goals such as retirement planning or buying a home require disciplined saving and investing over an extended period.

2. Tracking Progress

Monitoring progress toward financial goals can reinforce positive behaviors and provide a sense of accomplishment:

- Regular Reviews: Periodically reviewing financial goals and adjusting strategies as needed can ensure continued progress.

- Celebrating Milestones: Recognizing and celebrating milestones can maintain motivation and commitment to financial plans.

The Psychological Benefits of Saving and Investing

1. Financial Security

Effective saving and investing can provide a sense of financial security, reducing stress and anxiety about the future:

- Peace of Mind: Knowing that one has a financial cushion for emergencies and long-term needs can enhance overall well-being.

2. Empowerment

Taking control of one's financial future through disciplined saving and investing can foster a sense of empowerment and self-efficacy:

- Confidence: Achieving financial goals can build confidence and encourage further positive financial behaviors.

Conclusion

The psychology of saving and investing encompasses a range of factors, including delayed gratification, risk tolerance, cognitive biases, and the development of effective habits. By understanding these psychological influences, individuals can make more informed and rational financial decisions, ultimately achieving greater financial well-being. This chapter has explored the mindset and behaviors that contribute to successful saving and investing, highlighting strategies to enhance financial discipline and achieve long-term financial goals. As we continue to delve into the psychology of money, recognizing and addressing these psychological aspects will be essential for fostering healthier financial behaviors and building a secure financial future.

CHAPTER 12

THE IMPACT OF DEBT ON MENTAL HEALTH

Debt is a common financial reality for many people, but it can also be a significant source of stress and anxiety. The psychological burden of debt can profoundly affect mental health and overall well-being. This chapter explores the impact of debt on mental health, examining how it can lead to stress, anxiety, depression, and other psychological issues. It also discusses strategies for managing debt-related stress and improving financial and mental well-being.

The Psychological Burden of Debt

1. Stress and Anxiety

Debt can be a significant source of stress and anxiety, particularly when individuals struggle to make payments or face high interest rates. The constant worry about finances can lead to:

- Chronic Stress: Persistent financial stress can become chronic, impacting physical health by contributing to conditions such as hypertension and cardiovascular disease.

- Anxiety Disorders: The uncertainty and pressure of debt can trigger or exacerbate anxiety disorders, leading to symptoms such as excessive worry, restlessness, and difficulty concentrating.

2. Depression

Debt is closely linked to depression. The feelings of hopelessness and despair associated with overwhelming debt can contribute to:

- Clinical Depression: Individuals with significant debt may experience symptoms of clinical depression, including persistent sadness, loss of interest in activities, and changes in sleep and appetite.

- Low Self-Esteem: The stigma and shame associated with debt can lead to low self-esteem and feelings of inadequacy, further contributing to depressive symptoms.

3. Impact on Relationships

Debt can strain personal relationships, leading to conflicts and emotional distress:

- Marital Strain: Financial problems are a common source of tension in marriages and can lead to arguments, resentment, and even divorce.

- Social Isolation: The stigma of debt may cause individuals to withdraw from social activities and support networks, leading to feelings of isolation and loneliness.

Factors Influencing the Psychological Impact of Debt

1. Debt Type and Amount

The type and amount of debt can influence its psychological impact:

- High-Interest Debt: Credit card debt and payday loans with high interest rates can be particularly stressful due to the rapid accumulation of interest and fees.

- Secured vs. Unsecured Debt: Secured debt (e.g., mortgages, car loans) may be less stressful than unsecured debt (e.g., credit cards, personal loans) due to the potential for asset loss and higher interest rates.

2. Financial Literacy

Financial literacy can affect how individuals perceive and manage debt:

- Understanding Debt: Individuals with higher financial literacy may better understand debt management strategies and feel more in control of their financial situation.

- Mismanagement: Lack of financial knowledge can lead to poor debt management, exacerbating stress and anxiety.

3. Coping Mechanisms

The ways in which individuals cope with debt can influence its impact on mental health:

- Effective Coping: Seeking professional advice, creating a debt repayment plan, and using positive coping strategies can mitigate the psychological impact of debt.

- Maladaptive Coping: Avoiding the problem, using alcohol or drugs, or engaging in impulsive spending can worsen financial and mental health issues.

Strategies for Managing Debt-Related Stress

1. Financial Planning and Management

Developing a clear financial plan can help reduce debt-related stress:

- Budgeting: Creating and sticking to a budget can help individuals manage their finances more effectively and allocate funds toward debt repayment.

- Debt Repayment Strategies: Employing strategies such as the debt snowball or debt avalanche methods can provide structure and motivation for paying down debt.

2. Seeking Professional Help

Professional advice can be invaluable in managing debt and reducing stress:

- Credit Counseling: Credit counselors can provide guidance on managing debt, creating budgets, and negotiating with creditors.

- Financial Advisors: Financial advisors can offer personalized advice on debt management and overall financial planning.

3. Emotional and Mental Health Support

Addressing the emotional and psychological aspects of debt is crucial for overall well-being:

- Therapy and Counseling: Speaking with a therapist or counselor can help individuals cope with the emotional impact of debt and develop healthier coping strategies.

- Support Groups: Joining support groups for individuals dealing with debt can provide a sense of community and reduce feelings of isolation.

4. Building Financial Resilience

Building financial resilience can help individuals manage debt more effectively and reduce stress:

- Emergency Fund: Establishing an emergency fund can provide a financial safety net and reduce anxiety about unexpected expenses.

- Income Diversification: Exploring additional income streams, such as part-time work or freelancing, can provide financial stability and reduce reliance on debt.

5. Mindfulness and Stress Reduction Techniques

Incorporating mindfulness and stress reduction techniques can improve mental health and well-being:

- Mindfulness Practices: Techniques such as meditation, deep breathing, and yoga can help reduce stress and promote emotional balance.

- Physical Activity: Regular exercise can improve mood, reduce anxiety, and enhance overall mental health.

The Role of Societal and Policy Interventions

1. Financial Education Programs

Implementing financial education programs can empower individuals with the knowledge and skills needed to manage debt effectively:

- School Curricula: Integrating financial literacy into school curricula can provide young people with a strong foundation in money management.

- Community Workshops: Offering community-based financial education workshops can reach diverse populations and provide practical advice on managing debt.

2. Debt Relief Programs

Government and nonprofit organizations can offer debt relief programs to support individuals struggling with debt:

- Debt Consolidation: Programs that consolidate multiple debts into a single loan with a lower interest rate can simplify repayment and reduce financial stress.

- Bankruptcy Protection: Providing clear information and access to bankruptcy protection can help individuals make informed decisions about managing insurmountable debt.

3. Regulation of Predatory Lending

Regulating predatory lending practices can protect consumers from high-interest loans and unfair debt collection practices:

- Interest Rate Caps: Implementing caps on interest rates for consumer loans can prevent excessive debt accumulation.

- Transparent Disclosures: Requiring clear and transparent disclosures of loan terms can help consumers make informed borrowing decisions.

Conclusion

Debt can have a profound impact on mental health, leading to stress, anxiety, depression, and strained relationships. Understanding the psychological burden of debt and implementing strategies for managing debt-related stress are crucial for improving financial and mental well-being. This chapter has explored the various ways in which debt affects mental health and offered practical strategies for coping with and managing debt. By addressing both the financial and emotional aspects of debt, individuals can work towards a healthier, more secure financial future. As we continue to delve into the psychology of money, recognizing and addressing the impact of debt on mental health will be essential for fostering overall well-being and financial stability.

CHAPTER 13

FINANCIAL EDUCATION AND ITS IMPORTANCE

Financial literacy, the ability to understand and use various financial skills, is crucial for making informed financial decisions. It encompasses a range of knowledge, from budgeting and saving to investing and understanding credit. This chapter highlights the importance of financial education and its role in improving financial behavior and outcomes. It also explores the components of effective financial education and strategies for enhancing financial literacy across different demographics.

The Significance of Financial Education

1. Empowering Individuals

Financial education empowers individuals to take control of their financial lives. It equips them with the knowledge and skills needed to make sound financial decisions, ultimately leading to greater financial independence and security. Key benefits include:

- Improved Decision-Making: Financially literate individuals can make informed choices about spending, saving, borrowing, and investing.

- Increased Confidence: Understanding financial concepts builds confidence in managing money and navigating financial products and services.

2. Preventing Financial Mistakes

Lack of financial literacy can lead to costly mistakes and poor financial outcomes. Educating individuals about basic financial principles helps prevent issues such as:

- Excessive Debt: Understanding interest rates and credit terms can prevent individuals from accumulating unmanageable debt.

- Insufficient Savings: Knowledge of budgeting and the importance of saving can encourage individuals to build emergency funds and plan for future needs.

3. Promoting Economic Stability

At a broader level, financial education contributes to economic stability and growth. When individuals manage their finances well, it can lead to:

- Higher Savings Rates: Increased personal savings can provide more capital for investment and economic development.

- Reduced Financial Stress: Financially secure individuals are less likely to experience the stress and health issues associated with financial instability, leading to a healthier, more productive workforce.

Components of Effective Financial Education

1. Basic Financial Concepts

Effective financial education should cover the foundational concepts necessary for managing money, including:

- Budgeting: Understanding how to create and maintain a budget to manage income and expenses.

- Saving: The importance of saving for emergencies, future goals, and retirement.

- Credit and Debt Management: Knowledge of how credit works, the impact of interest rates, and strategies for managing and reducing debt.

2. Advanced Financial Skills

Beyond the basics, financial education should also address more advanced topics to help individuals grow their wealth and achieve long-term financial goals:

- Investing: Understanding different types of investments, risk and return, and the principles of diversification.

- Retirement Planning: The importance of saving for retirement, the benefits of different retirement accounts, and strategies for building a retirement fund.

- Tax Planning: Basic knowledge of how taxes work and strategies for minimizing tax liabilities.

3. Behavioral Finance

Incorporating behavioral finance principles into financial education can help individuals recognize and mitigate cognitive biases and emotional influences on their financial decisions:

- Cognitive Biases: Understanding common biases such as overconfidence, loss aversion, and the anchoring effect.

- Emotional Influences: Recognizing how emotions such as fear, greed, and regret can impact financial behavior.

Strategies for Enhancing Financial Literacy

1. Integrating Financial Education into School Curricula

Introducing financial education at an early age can lay the foundation for lifelong financial literacy:

- Primary and Secondary Education: Incorporating financial literacy lessons into the standard curriculum can help students develop essential money management skills.

- Higher Education: Offering personal finance courses at colleges and universities can prepare young adults for financial independence and decision-making.

2. Community-Based Financial Education Programs

Community programs can reach a broad audience and provide practical financial education tailored to specific needs:

- Workshops and Seminars: Organizing local workshops and seminars on various financial topics can engage community members and provide valuable knowledge.

- Partnerships with Nonprofits: Collaborating with nonprofit organizations to deliver financial education can enhance outreach and impact, especially in underserved communities.

3. Utilizing Technology and Digital Platforms

Technology can expand access to financial education and provide interactive, engaging learning experiences:

- Online Courses and Webinars: Offering online courses and webinars on financial topics can make education more accessible and flexible.

- Mobile Apps: Developing mobile apps that provide financial education, budgeting tools, and personalized advice can help individuals manage their finances on the go.

- Social Media and Blogs: Leveraging social media and blogs to share financial tips, articles, and resources can reach a wider audience and promote financial literacy.

4. Employer-Sponsored Financial Education

Employers can play a significant role in promoting financial literacy by offering financial education programs to their employees:

- Workplace Workshops: Hosting workshops on topics such as retirement planning, investing, and debt management can help employees make informed financial decisions.

- Financial Wellness Programs: Implementing comprehensive financial wellness programs that include education, counseling, and resources can enhance employees' financial well-being and productivity.

Addressing Financial Literacy Gaps

1. Targeting Underserved Populations

Certain populations may have limited access to financial education and resources, including low-income individuals, minorities, and immigrants. Strategies to address these gaps include:

- Culturally Relevant Education: Developing financial education materials and programs that are culturally relevant and accessible to diverse populations.

- Language Accessibility: Providing financial education resources in multiple languages to reach non-English-speaking individuals.

2. Tailoring Education to Different Life Stages

Financial needs and challenges vary across different life stages. Tailoring financial education to address these specific needs can enhance its effectiveness:

- Youth and Young Adults: Focus on basic money management skills, the importance of saving, and understanding credit.

- Midlife Adults: Emphasize retirement planning, investing, and managing debt.

- Seniors: Provide information on estate planning, healthcare costs, and managing retirement income.

3. Measuring and Evaluating Impact

Assessing the effectiveness of financial education programs is crucial for continuous improvement and ensuring positive outcomes:

- Pre- and Post-Assessments: Conducting assessments before and after financial education programs can measure knowledge gains and behavioral changes.

- Longitudinal Studies: Implementing longitudinal studies to track the long-term impact of financial education on individuals' financial behavior and well-being.

The Future of Financial Education

1. Innovative Approaches

The future of financial education lies in embracing innovative approaches and technologies to enhance learning experiences:

- Gamification: Using gamification techniques to make financial education more engaging and interactive can improve knowledge retention and application.
- Virtual Reality (VR): Incorporating VR experiences to simulate real-life financial decisions can provide hands-on learning opportunities.

2. Collaboration and Partnerships

Collaboration between various stakeholders, including governments, educational institutions, nonprofits, and the private sector, is essential for promoting financial literacy:

- Public-Private Partnerships: Leveraging resources and expertise from both public and private sectors can expand the reach and impact of financial education initiatives.
- Global Initiatives: Participating in global initiatives and sharing best practices can enhance financial literacy efforts worldwide.

Conclusion

Financial education is a vital tool for empowering individuals to make informed financial decisions, prevent costly mistakes, and achieve long-term financial security. By understanding and addressing the components of effective financial education, we can enhance financial literacy across different demographics and promote economic stability. This chapter has highlighted the importance of financial education, explored strategies for improving financial literacy, and discussed innovative approaches and future directions. As we continue to delve into the psychology of money, prioritizing financial education will be essential for fostering healthier financial behaviors and improving overall well-being.

CHAPTER 14

STRATEGIES FOR BETTER FINANCIAL DECISIONS

Making sound financial decisions is crucial for achieving financial well-being and long-term security. By drawing on insights from psychology and behavioral economics, individuals can develop strategies to improve their financial decision-making. This chapter offers practical strategies for setting financial goals, budgeting, and employing decision-making techniques to enhance financial well-being.

Goal Setting

1. Importance of Goal Setting

Setting clear financial goals provides direction and motivation for managing money effectively. Goals help individuals prioritize their spending, saving, and investing efforts, leading to better financial outcomes.

2. SMART Goals

Effective financial goals should be SMART: Specific, Measurable, Achievable, Relevant, and Time-bound:

- Specific: Clearly define what you want to achieve. For example, "Save $10,000 for a down payment on a house."

- Measurable: Ensure the goal can be tracked and measured. For example, "Save $200 per month."

- Achievable: Set realistic goals based on your current financial situation. For example, "Save $200 per month" is more achievable than "Save $1,000 per month" if your income is limited.

- Relevant: Align your goals with your broader financial objectives and values. For example, saving for a house is relevant if homeownership is important to you.

- Time-bound: Set a deadline for achieving your goal. For example, "Save $10,000 in five years."

3. Short-Term and Long-Term Goals

Balancing short-term and long-term goals is essential for comprehensive financial planning:

- Short-Term Goals: Goals that can be achieved within a year, such as saving for a vacation or paying off a credit card.

- Long-Term Goals: Goals that take several years to achieve, such as saving for retirement or buying a house.

4. Tracking Progress

Regularly monitoring and tracking progress toward financial goals can help maintain motivation and make necessary adjustments:

- Financial Journals: Keeping a financial journal to record income, expenses, and progress toward goals.
- Digital Tools: Using apps and online tools to track savings, investments, and other financial metrics.

Budgeting

1. Creating a Budget

A budget is a fundamental tool for managing finances effectively. It helps individuals allocate income toward expenses, savings, and investments:

- Income: Calculate total monthly income from all sources.
- Expenses: List all monthly expenses, including fixed expenses (e.g., rent, utilities) and variable expenses (e.g., groceries, entertainment).
- Savings and Investments: Allocate a portion of income toward savings and investments.
- Balance: Ensure that total expenses and savings do not exceed income.

2. Budgeting Methods

Different budgeting methods can help individuals manage their finances based on their preferences and goals:

- Zero-Based Budgeting: Allocate every dollar of income to specific expenses, savings, or debt repayment, ensuring that income minus expenses equals zero.
- 50/30/20 Rule: Allocate 50% of income to needs, 30% to wants, and 20% to savings and debt repayment.
- Envelope System: Use cash envelopes for different spending categories to control discretionary spending.

3. Adjusting the Budget

Regularly reviewing and adjusting the budget is crucial for staying on track with financial goals:

- Monthly Reviews: Conduct monthly reviews to compare actual spending with the budget and make necessary adjustments.
- Flexible Adjustments: Adjust the budget as needed to accommodate changes in income, expenses, or financial priorities.

Decision-Making Techniques

1. Behavioral Insights

Applying behavioral insights can help individuals make better financial decisions by addressing cognitive biases and emotional influences:

- Nudging: Implementing small changes in the environment to encourage positive financial behaviors, such as setting up automatic savings transfers.

- Framing: Presenting financial information in a way that highlights the benefits of positive behaviors, such as emphasizing the long-term growth of investments.

2. Decision-Making Frameworks

Using structured decision-making frameworks can improve the quality of financial decisions:

- Cost-Benefit Analysis: Evaluating the potential costs and benefits of different financial options to make informed choices.

- Pros and Cons List: Listing the pros and cons of a financial decision to weigh the potential outcomes.

3. Avoiding Common Pitfalls

Being aware of common decision-making pitfalls can help individuals avoid mistakes:

- Overconfidence: Recognizing the limits of one's knowledge and seeking professional advice when needed.

- Herd Behavior: Avoiding the temptation to follow the crowd without conducting independent research.

- Anchoring: Being mindful of initial reference points and evaluating financial decisions based on current information.

Enhancing Financial Well-Being

1. Building an Emergency Fund

An emergency fund provides a financial safety net for unexpected expenses, reducing stress and promoting financial stability:

- Savings Target: Aim to save three to six months' worth of living expenses.
- Regular Contributions: Set up automatic transfers to a dedicated emergency fund account.

2. Debt Management

Effective debt management strategies can help individuals reduce financial stress and improve financial health:

- Debt Repayment Plans: Implement debt repayment strategies such as the debt snowball (paying off smallest debts first) or debt avalanche (paying off debts with the highest interest rates first).
- Debt Consolidation: Consider consolidating high-interest debts into a single loan with a lower interest rate.

3. Investing for the Future

Investing is essential for building wealth and achieving long-term financial goals:

- Diversification: Diversify investments across different asset classes to manage risk.

- Regular Contributions: Make regular contributions to investment accounts, such as retirement accounts and brokerage accounts.

- Long-Term Perspective: Maintain a long-term perspective and avoid making impulsive investment decisions based on short-term market fluctuations.

4. Continuous Financial Education

Continuous financial education is vital for staying informed about financial markets, products, and strategies:

- Reading Books and Articles: Regularly read books, articles, and blogs on personal finance and investing.

- Attending Workshops and Seminars: Participate in financial workshops and seminars to learn from experts and gain new insights.

- Seeking Professional Advice: Consult with financial advisors to receive personalized advice and stay updated on financial trends.

Conclusion

Making better financial decisions is essential for achieving financial well-being and long-term security. By setting clear financial goals, creating and adjusting budgets, and using structured decision-making techniques, individuals can improve their financial behaviors and outcomes. Drawing on insights from psychology and behavioral economics, this chapter has provided practical strategies for enhancing financial decision-making. As we continue to explore the psychology of money, adopting these strategies will be crucial for fostering healthier financial habits and achieving financial success.

CHAPTER 15

THE FUTURE OF FINANCIAL BEHAVIOR

The field of financial behavior is continuously evolving, driven by advancements in technology, changes in societal norms, and new insights from research. Emerging trends and technologies such as financial technology (fintech), artificial intelligence (AI), and blockchain are reshaping the way individuals manage their finances and make financial decisions. This chapter explores these developments and their potential impact on financial behavior and decision-making.

The Rise of Fintech

1. Definition and Scope

Fintech refers to the integration of technology into offerings by financial services companies to improve their use and delivery to consumers. It encompasses a wide range of applications, including mobile banking, online payments, and investment platforms.

2. Impact on Financial Behavior

Fintech has significantly impacted financial behavior in several ways:

- Accessibility: Fintech has made financial services more accessible to a broader audience, including underserved populations. Mobile banking apps and online platforms allow individuals to manage their finances anytime, anywhere.

- Convenience: The convenience of fintech solutions has simplified financial tasks such as budgeting, transferring money, and investing, encouraging more proactive financial management.

- Transparency: Fintech platforms often provide users with real-time data and analytics, increasing transparency and helping users make more informed decisions.

3. Popular Fintech Innovations

Several fintech innovations are particularly influential in shaping financial behavior:

- Robo-Advisors: Automated investment platforms that use algorithms to provide financial advice and manage portfolios. They offer low-cost, personalized investment management.

- Peer-to-Peer Lending: Online platforms that connect borrowers with individual lenders, often at lower interest rates than traditional banks.

- Cryptocurrencies and Blockchain: Digital currencies and blockchain technology offer decentralized, secure ways to conduct transactions and manage assets.

Artificial Intelligence and Machine Learning

1. Role in Financial Services

AI and machine learning are transforming financial services by enabling more sophisticated data analysis, predictive modeling, and personalized recommendations:

- Risk Assessment: AI can analyze vast amounts of data to assess credit risk and detect fraudulent activities more accurately.

- Personalized Financial Advice: Machine learning algorithms can analyze individual financial behaviors and preferences to provide tailored financial advice and product recommendations.

2. Impact on Financial Behavior

AI and machine learning are changing how individuals interact with financial services and make decisions:

- Enhanced Decision-Making: AI-driven tools provide insights and recommendations based on comprehensive data analysis, helping individuals make better-informed financial decisions.

- Behavioral Nudges: AI can identify patterns in financial behavior and deliver personalized nudges to encourage positive financial habits, such as saving more or spending less.

3. Challenges and Considerations

While AI and machine learning offer significant benefits, they also present challenges:

- Data Privacy: The use of personal financial data by AI systems raises concerns about privacy and data security.

- Bias and Fairness: Ensuring that AI algorithms are free from bias and provide fair recommendations to all users is critical.

Blockchain and Cryptocurrencies

1. Blockchain Technology

Blockchain is a decentralized ledger technology that enables secure, transparent, and tamper-proof transactions. It underpins cryptocurrencies like Bitcoin and Ethereum:

- Transparency and Security: Blockchain's transparency and security features make it an attractive option for various financial applications, from transactions to contract management.

2. Cryptocurrencies

Cryptocurrencies are digital or virtual currencies that use cryptography for security. They offer an alternative to traditional fiat currencies and banking systems:

- Decentralization: Cryptocurrencies operate on decentralized networks, reducing reliance on central banks and financial institutions.

- Investment Opportunities: Cryptocurrencies have emerged as a new asset class, offering opportunities for investment and diversification.

3. Impact on Financial Behavior

Blockchain and cryptocurrencies are influencing financial behavior in several ways:

- Increased Adoption: As cryptocurrencies become more widely accepted, individuals are incorporating them into their financial portfolios and transaction activities.

- Financial Inclusion: Blockchain technology can provide financial services to individuals in regions with limited access to traditional banking, promoting financial inclusion.

4. Challenges and Risks

The adoption of blockchain and cryptocurrencies comes with challenges and risks:

- Volatility: Cryptocurrencies are known for their price volatility, which can lead to significant financial gains or losses.

- Regulatory Uncertainty: The regulatory environment for cryptocurrencies is still evolving, creating uncertainty for users and investors.

Behavioral Insights and Digital Platforms

1. Behavioral Finance Applications

Digital platforms are increasingly incorporating behavioral finance principles to help users make better financial decisions:

- Gamification: Using game-like elements, such as rewards and challenges, to motivate positive financial behaviors, such as saving or paying down debt.
- Behavioral Nudges: Delivering personalized nudges based on user behavior to encourage beneficial financial actions, such as increasing retirement contributions.

2. Impact on Financial Literacy

Digital platforms can enhance financial literacy by providing educational resources and interactive tools:

- Educational Content: Many fintech apps offer articles, videos, and tutorials on various financial topics to help users improve their financial knowledge.
- Simulations and Tools: Interactive tools and simulations, such as retirement calculators and budget planners, help users understand the impact of their financial decisions.

3. Community and Peer Influence

Online communities and social networks play a significant role in financial behavior:

- Peer Sharing: Platforms that allow users to share financial goals and progress can create a sense of community and accountability.
- Social Trading: Social trading platforms enable users to follow and copy the trades of successful investors, leveraging peer influence to improve investment outcomes.

The Role of Government and Regulation

1. Regulatory Frameworks

As financial technologies evolve, governments and regulatory bodies play a crucial role in ensuring consumer protection and market stability:

- Regulating Fintech: Implementing regulations that protect consumers while promoting innovation in the fintech sector.
- Cryptocurrency Regulations: Developing clear regulatory frameworks for cryptocurrencies to address issues such as fraud, money laundering, and investor protection.

2. Promoting Financial Inclusion

Governments can leverage technology to promote financial inclusion and ensure that all individuals have access to financial services:

- Digital Identity: Implementing digital identity solutions to enable access to financial services for underserved populations.

- Public-Private Partnerships: Collaborating with fintech companies to develop and implement financial inclusion initiatives.

Future Trends and Predictions

1. Integration of AI and Blockchain

The integration of AI and blockchain technology has the potential to revolutionize financial services:

- Smart Contracts: AI-powered smart contracts on blockchain can automate complex financial transactions and agreements, reducing the need for intermediaries.

- Predictive Analytics: Combining AI with blockchain data can enhance predictive analytics for investment and risk management.

2. Enhanced Personalization

Advancements in data analytics and machine learning will enable even greater personalization of financial services:

- Tailored Financial Products: Financial institutions will offer more customized products and services based on individual financial behaviors and preferences.

- Real-Time Financial Management: AI-driven platforms will provide real-time insights and recommendations, helping users make proactive financial decisions.

3. Sustainable Finance

The future of financial behavior will increasingly focus on sustainability and ethical considerations:

- Green Investments: Growing awareness of environmental issues will drive demand for sustainable investment options, such as green bonds and ESG (Environmental, Social, and Governance) funds.

- Impact Investing: Investors will seek opportunities that generate positive social and environmental impact alongside financial returns.

Conclusion

The future of financial behavior is being shaped by rapid advancements in technology, emerging trends, and evolving societal norms. Fintech, AI, blockchain, and cryptocurrencies are transforming how individuals manage their finances and make financial decisions. By understanding and leveraging these developments, individuals can improve their financial well-being and adapt to the changing financial landscape. This chapter has explored the potential impact of these technologies and trends on financial behavior, highlighting the opportunities and challenges they present. As we continue to navigate the evolving world of finance, staying informed and adaptable will be key to achieving financial success and security.

CHAPTER 16

WHY US CONSUMERS THINK THE WAY THEY THINK

Understanding the mindset of US consumers is crucial for businesses, policymakers, and financial advisors. The way US consumers think and make financial decisions is influenced by a complex interplay of cultural, social, economic, and psychological factors. This chapter delves into these influences to explain why US consumers behave the way they do, examining the role of individualism, consumer culture, economic environment, and psychological principles in shaping consumer behavior.

Cultural Influences

1. Individualism

One of the most significant cultural influences on US consumers is individualism, a core American value that emphasizes personal freedom, self-reliance, and individual achievement. This value shapes consumer behavior in several ways:

- Self-Expression: US consumers often use their purchasing decisions to express their individuality and personal identity. This can be seen in the popularity of customized products and brands that emphasize uniqueness.

- Personal Responsibility: The belief in personal responsibility leads consumers to prioritize self-sufficiency and financial independence, influencing their saving and investment behaviors.

2. Materialism

Materialism, the importance placed on acquiring and owning material goods, is another prominent cultural influence in the US. This drives consumer behavior in multiple ways:

- Status Symbols: Consumers often purchase high-end products and luxury brands to signal social status and success.

- Consumerism: The constant pursuit of new and better products fuels a culture of consumption, encouraging frequent spending and the accumulation of goods.

3. Work Ethic

The American work ethic, characterized by a strong belief in hard work and its rewards, also impacts consumer behavior:

- Disposable Income: High levels of work and income often result in increased disposable income, which can drive higher levels of consumption.

- Reward Spending: Many consumers view spending as a reward for their hard work, leading to indulgent purchases and luxury spending.

Social Influences

1. Peer Influence

Social interactions and peer pressure significantly shape consumer behavior in the US:

- Social Comparison: Consumers frequently compare themselves to their peers, leading to spending behaviors aimed at keeping up with or surpassing others.

- Peer Recommendations: Word-of-mouth and peer recommendations play a crucial role in purchasing decisions, with consumers often relying on the opinions of friends and family.

2. Media and Advertising

The media and advertising industries have a profound impact on consumer behavior:

- Advertising Exposure: Constant exposure to advertisements shapes consumer desires and perceptions of needs versus wants.

- Influencer Culture: Social media influencers and celebrities can heavily influence purchasing decisions, promoting products and lifestyles that consumers aspire to emulate.

3. Socioeconomic Status

Socioeconomic status influences consumer behavior by shaping access to resources and financial priorities:

- Income Levels: Higher income levels typically correlate with higher spending power and different consumption patterns compared to lower income levels.

- Financial Priorities: Consumers from different socioeconomic backgrounds may prioritize spending, saving, and investing differently based on their financial goals and constraints.

Economic Influences

1. Economic Environment

The broader economic environment, including factors such as inflation, interest rates, and employment levels, significantly affects consumer behavior:

- Economic Cycles: During economic downturns, consumers tend to be more cautious with their spending, while economic booms often lead to increased consumption.

- Inflation and Interest Rates: High inflation and interest rates can deter spending and borrowing, while low rates can encourage both.

2. Credit Availability

The availability of credit plays a crucial role in shaping consumer behavior:

- Credit Cards: Easy access to credit cards enables consumers to spend beyond their immediate means, often leading to higher levels of debt.

- Loans and Financing: The availability of financing options for large purchases, such as homes and cars, influences consumers' ability to make significant investments.

3. Employment and Income Stability

Employment status and income stability are key determinants of consumer confidence and spending behavior:

- Job Security: Stable employment and reliable income sources increase consumer confidence, leading to higher levels of spending.

- Unemployment: Conversely, unemployment or underemployment leads to reduced spending and increased saving as consumers prioritize financial security.

Psychological Influences

1. Cognitive Biases

Cognitive biases influence how US consumers make financial decisions:

- Overconfidence: Overconfidence can lead consumers to make risky financial decisions, such as excessive borrowing or speculative investments.

- Anchoring: The tendency to rely heavily on the first piece of information encountered (the "anchor") can affect purchasing decisions, such as relying on the initial price of a product as a reference point.

2. Emotional Factors

Emotions play a significant role in consumer behavior:

- Impulse Buying: Emotions such as excitement, stress, or boredom can lead to impulse purchases, where consumers buy items spontaneously without thorough consideration.

- Retail Therapy: Shopping is often used as a way to cope with negative emotions, providing a temporary boost in mood.

3. Behavioral Economics

Insights from behavioral economics explain how psychological factors impact financial decisions:

- Nudging: Small changes in the environment, or "nudges," can encourage positive financial behaviors, such as saving more or spending less.

- Loss Aversion: The tendency to prefer avoiding losses over acquiring equivalent gains can influence decisions, such as holding onto losing investments for too long.

Technological Influences

1. E-Commerce and Digital Platforms

The rise of e-commerce and digital platforms has transformed consumer behavior:

- Convenience: The convenience of online shopping has increased consumer spending, as it is easier to make purchases from anywhere at any time.

- Personalization: Digital platforms use data analytics to offer personalized recommendations, enhancing the shopping experience and encouraging more purchases.

2. Mobile Technology

Mobile technology has further influenced consumer behavior:

- Mobile Payments: The adoption of mobile payment solutions, such as Apple Pay and Google Wallet, has streamlined transactions and increased spending.

- Shopping Apps: Mobile shopping apps provide users with easy access to products and promotions, facilitating impulse buying and frequent shopping.

3. Social Media

Social media has a profound impact on consumer behavior:

- Influencer Marketing: Social media influencers play a significant role in shaping consumer preferences and purchasing decisions through endorsements and sponsored content.

- User-Generated Content: Reviews, ratings, and user-generated content on social media platforms influence consumer trust and decisions.

Strategies for Influencing US Consumer Behavior

1. Marketing Strategies

Businesses can leverage insights into consumer behavior to develop effective marketing strategies:

- Targeted Advertising: Using data analytics to deliver targeted advertisements that resonate with specific consumer segments.

- Emotional Appeals: Creating advertisements that evoke emotions can strengthen brand connections and influence purchasing decisions.

2. Product Development

Understanding consumer behavior can inform product development:

- Customization: Offering customizable products that allow consumers to express their individuality.
- Sustainability: Developing sustainable products to meet the growing demand for environmentally friendly options.

3. Customer Engagement

Engaging with consumers through various channels can enhance loyalty and influence behavior:

- Social Media Interaction: Actively engaging with consumers on social media platforms to build relationships and gather feedback.
- Loyalty Programs: Implementing loyalty programs that reward repeat customers and encourage long-term engagement.

Conclusion

US consumers' financial decisions are shaped by a complex interplay of cultural, social, economic, psychological, and technological factors. Understanding these influences can help businesses, policymakers, and financial advisors tailor their strategies to better meet the needs and preferences of US consumers. This chapter has explored the various factors that influence why US consumers think and behave the way they do, highlighting the importance of considering these factors in developing effective marketing, product development, and customer engagement strategies. As we continue to study the psychology of money, recognizing and addressing these influences will be essential for fostering healthier financial behaviors and improving overall financial well-being.

CHAPTER 17

THE DISTINCTION BETWEEN GETTING WEALTHY AND STAYING WEALTHY

Achieving wealth is a significant milestone, but maintaining that wealth over the long term requires a different set of skills and behaviors. This chapter explores the distinction between getting wealthy and staying wealthy, examining the strategies, mindset, and habits necessary for not only accumulating wealth but also preserving and growing it over time.

The Path to Wealth

1. Earning

The first step to getting wealthy typically involves increasing one's earning potential. Key factors include:

- Education and Skills: Higher education and specialized skills often lead to better-paying jobs and career advancement opportunities.

- Entrepreneurship: Starting and growing a successful business can be a path to substantial wealth, albeit with higher risks.

- Investments: Making strategic investments in stocks, real estate, or other assets can generate additional income and capital gains.

2. Saving and Investing

Accumulating wealth requires disciplined saving and strategic investing:

- Saving: Consistently saving a portion of income is crucial for building a financial foundation.

- Investing: Investing savings in growth-oriented assets such as stocks, real estate, and mutual funds helps to increase wealth over time through capital appreciation and dividends.

3. Risk-Taking

Getting wealthy often involves a certain level of risk-taking:

- Investment Risk: Investing in volatile or high-growth opportunities can lead to significant returns but also carries the risk of losses.

- Entrepreneurial Risk: Starting a business involves risks such as market competition, financial instability, and potential failure.

The Mindset for Getting Wealthy

1. Goal-Oriented

Successful wealth builders are typically very goal-oriented:

- Clear Goals: Setting specific, measurable financial goals provides direction and motivation.
- Long-Term Vision: Maintaining a long-term perspective helps individuals stay focused on their ultimate objectives.

2. Proactive and Opportunistic

Wealth accumulators are often proactive and opportunistic:

- Seizing Opportunities: They are willing to take calculated risks to seize investment and business opportunities.
- Continuous Learning: Staying informed about market trends and continuously seeking new knowledge and skills is essential for capitalizing on opportunities.

The Path to Staying Wealthy

1. Preserving Wealth

Staying wealthy involves a strong focus on preserving accumulated wealth:

- Risk Management: Implementing strategies to manage and mitigate risks is crucial for wealth preservation.
- Diversification: Diversifying investments across different asset classes reduces exposure to any single investment's volatility and risk.

2. Prudent Spending

Wealth maintenance requires prudent spending habits:

- Lifestyle Inflation: Avoiding significant lifestyle inflation ensures that increased income does not lead to proportionally higher expenses.
- Budgeting: Maintaining a budget helps manage expenses and prevents overspending.

3. Long-Term Investing

Long-term investing is essential for sustaining wealth:

- Compound Growth: Investing with a long-term horizon allows for compound growth, which significantly increases wealth over time.
- Stable Investments: Allocating a portion of wealth to stable, income-generating investments such as bonds and dividend-paying stocks provides steady returns.

The Mindset for Staying Wealthy

1. Conservative and Risk-Averse

The mindset for staying wealthy often involves a more conservative and risk-averse approach compared to the mindset for getting wealthy:

- Risk Aversion: Focusing on preserving capital rather than seeking high-risk, high-reward opportunities.
- Caution: Making cautious, well-researched investment decisions to protect wealth.

2. Disciplined and Patient

Staying wealthy requires discipline and patience:

- Consistency: Adhering to a consistent investment strategy and avoiding impulsive decisions based on market fluctuations.
- Patience: Understanding that wealth preservation and growth take time and resisting the urge to chase quick gains.

3. Adaptability and Resilience

Adaptability and resilience are crucial for maintaining wealth in the face of changing economic conditions:

- Economic Changes: Being prepared to adapt to economic shifts, such as recessions or changes in tax policies, to protect wealth.
- Resilience: Building resilience through diversification and maintaining a strong financial foundation to weather financial setbacks.

Strategies for Transitioning from Getting Wealthy to Staying Wealthy

1. Reevaluating Goals and Strategies

As individuals transition from getting wealthy to staying wealthy, it is important to reevaluate goals and strategies:

- Goal Adjustment: Shifting focus from aggressive wealth accumulation to wealth preservation and steady growth.
- Strategy Realignment: Adjusting investment strategies to align with new goals, such as increasing allocations to stable, income-generating assets.

2. Estate Planning

Estate planning is essential for ensuring the longevity of wealth:

- Wills and Trusts: Creating wills and trusts to manage the distribution of assets and minimize tax liabilities.
- Succession Planning: Planning for the succession of businesses and investments to ensure they continue to generate wealth for future generations.

3. Continuous Monitoring and Adaptation

Regularly monitoring financial health and adapting strategies as needed is crucial for staying wealthy:

- Financial Reviews: Conduct regular financial reviews to assess the performance of investments and make necessary adjustments.

- Adapting to Change: Staying informed about changes in the economic landscape and adapting strategies to protect and grow wealth.

The Role of Financial Advisors

1. Expert Guidance

Financial advisors can provide expert guidance for both getting and staying wealthy:

- Investment Advice: Offering personalized investment advice based on individual risk tolerance and financial goals.

- Tax Planning: Providing strategies to minimize tax liabilities and maximize after-tax returns.

2. Wealth Management

Wealth management services can help individuals transition from wealth accumulation to wealth preservation:

- Comprehensive Planning: Developing comprehensive financial plans that address all aspects of wealth management, including investing, estate planning, and risk management.

- Ongoing Support: Offering ongoing support and advice to help individuals adapt to changing financial circumstances.

Common Pitfalls to Avoid

1. Overconfidence and Recklessness

Overconfidence can lead to reckless financial decisions that jeopardize wealth:

- High-Risk Investments: Avoid unnecessary high-risk investments that do not align with long-term wealth preservation goals.
- Impulsive Spending: Steering clear of impulsive spending that can erode wealth over time.

2. Neglecting Risk Management

Failing to manage risks effectively can lead to significant financial losses:

- Lack of Diversification: Ensuring investments are diversified to reduce exposure to market volatility.
- Underestimating Market Cycles: Being aware of market cycles and preparing for downturns to protect wealth.

3. Ignoring Inflation and Taxes

Inflation and taxes can erode wealth if not properly managed:

- Inflation Protection: Investing in assets that provide protection against inflation, such as real estate and inflation-indexed bonds.

- Tax Efficiency: Implementing tax-efficient investment strategies to maximize after-tax returns.

Conclusion

The journey from getting wealthy to staying wealthy requires a shift in mindset, strategies, and behaviors. While accumulating wealth often involves risk-taking and aggressive growth strategies, preserving and growing that wealth over the long term requires prudence, discipline, and adaptability. This chapter has explored the key differences between getting wealthy and staying wealthy, highlighting the importance of goal setting, prudent spending, long-term investing, and effective risk management. By understanding and implementing these principles, individuals can achieve and maintain financial security and success.

CHAPTER 18

WEALTH IS NOT ALWAYS CONSPICUOUS

Wealth is often associated with visible signs of affluence, such as luxury cars, expensive homes, and designer clothing. However, true wealth is not always conspicuous and can often be hidden beneath a modest lifestyle. This chapter explores the concept that wealth is not always visible, examining the habits, attitudes, and strategies of individuals who build and maintain wealth discreetly. It also discusses the advantages of inconspicuous wealth and how it contributes to long-term financial stability and well-being.

The Concept of Inconspicuous Wealth

1. Definition

Inconspicuous wealth refers to financial prosperity that is not overtly displayed through material possessions or extravagant spending. Individuals with inconspicuous wealth often choose to live below their means and prioritize financial security over social status.

2. Characteristics

People with inconspicuous wealth typically exhibit certain characteristics:

- Frugality: They practice frugality and mindful spending, focusing on value rather than luxury.
- Savings and Investments: They prioritize saving and investing over spending on non-essential items.
- Modest Lifestyle: They maintain a modest lifestyle that does not reflect their true financial standing.

The Psychology Behind Inconspicuous Wealth

1. Values and Priorities

Individuals with inconspicuous wealth often have different values and priorities compared to those who display their wealth more visibly:

- Financial Independence: They value financial independence and security over public recognition or admiration.
- Long-Term Goals: They focus on long-term financial goals such as retirement planning, education funding, and generational wealth transfer.

- Personal Fulfillment: They derive satisfaction from personal achievements, relationships, and experiences rather than material possessions.

2. Avoiding Social Pressure

By choosing to live modestly, individuals with inconspicuous wealth can avoid the social pressures and expectations associated with visible wealth:

- Reduced Stress: Avoiding the pressure to keep up with peers or maintain a certain image can reduce stress and contribute to overall well-being.

- Privacy: Maintaining privacy about one's financial situation can protect against unwanted attention and financial solicitations.

Habits and Strategies of Inconspicuous Wealth Builders

1. Mindful Spending

Mindful spending is a key habit of those who build and maintain inconspicuous wealth:

- Needs vs. Wants: They distinguish between needs and wants, prioritizing essential expenses and carefully considering discretionary spending.

- Value-Oriented Purchases: They focus on purchasing high-quality items that offer long-term value rather than trendy or luxury products.

2. Consistent Saving and Investing

Regular saving and investing are fundamental strategies for building inconspicuous wealth:

- Automatic Savings: They often set up automatic transfers to savings and investment accounts to ensure consistent contributions.

- Diversified Investments: They maintain diversified investment portfolios to manage risk and achieve long-term growth.

3. Financial Education

Individuals with inconspicuous wealth typically prioritize financial education and literacy:

- Continuous Learning: They stay informed about financial markets, investment strategies, and personal finance principles.

- Professional Advice: They seek advice from financial advisors to optimize their financial plans and make informed decisions.

Advantages of Inconspicuous Wealth

1. Financial Security

One of the main advantages of inconspicuous wealth is enhanced financial security:

- Emergency Fund: They often maintain substantial emergency funds to cover unexpected expenses and provide peace of mind.

- Debt Avoidance: By living within their means, they can avoid high levels of debt and the associated financial stress.

2. Flexibility and Freedom

Inconspicuous wealth offers greater financial flexibility and freedom:

- Career Choices: They have the freedom to make career decisions based on personal fulfillment rather than financial necessity.

- Lifestyle Choices: They can choose lifestyles that align with their values and preferences without being constrained by financial pressures.

3. Long-Term Growth

By focusing on saving and investing, individuals with inconspicuous wealth can achieve significant long-term growth:

- Compound Interest: Consistent investing allows them to benefit from compound interest, leading to substantial wealth accumulation over time.

- Generational Wealth: They can build and transfer wealth to future generations, ensuring long-term financial stability for their families.

Case Studies of Inconspicuous Wealth

1. Warren Buffett

Warren Buffett, one of the wealthiest individuals in the world, is known for his modest lifestyle:

- Frugal Living: Despite his immense wealth, Buffett lives in the same house he bought in 1958 and avoids extravagant spending.
- Focus on Investments: He prioritizes investing and growing his wealth through Berkshire Hathaway, demonstrating the principles of inconspicuous wealth.

2. The Millionaire Next Door

Thomas J. Stanley and William D. Danko's book "The Millionaire Next Door" highlights the habits of inconspicuous millionaires:

- Modest Lifestyles: The book reveals that many millionaires live modestly, drive used cars, and focus on saving and investing.
- Wealth Accumulation: These individuals accumulate wealth through disciplined financial practices rather than high incomes or extravagant spending.

Implementing Inconspicuous Wealth Strategies

1. Adopting a Frugal Mindset

Adopting a frugal mindset is the first step toward building inconspicuous wealth:

- Mindful Consumption: Practice mindful consumption by evaluating purchases based on necessity and long-term value.

- Avoiding Lifestyle Inflation: Resist the temptation to increase spending with rising income, and maintain a modest lifestyle.

2. Prioritizing Savings and Investments

Consistent saving and investing are crucial for wealth accumulation:

- Automating Finances: Automate savings and investment contributions to ensure consistency and take advantage of dollar-cost averaging.

- Diversifying Investments: Build a diversified investment portfolio to manage risk and achieve steady growth.

3. Continuous Financial Education

Continuously educating yourself about personal finance and investing is essential for making informed decisions:

- Reading and Learning: Regularly read books, articles, and financial news to stay informed about market trends and financial strategies.

- Seeking Advice: Consult with financial advisors to optimize your financial plans and address any concerns.

Overcoming Challenges of Inconspicuous Wealth

1. Social Pressure

Overcoming social pressure to conform to visible displays of wealth can be challenging:

- Confidence in Choices: Develop confidence in your financial choices and focus on long-term goals rather than societal expectations.

- Support Networks: Surround yourself with like-minded individuals who share your values and support your financial decisions.

2. Maintaining Discipline

Maintaining discipline in saving and investing requires consistent effort and commitment:

- Setting Goals: Set clear financial goals and regularly review your progress to stay motivated.

- Building Habits: Establish strong financial habits, such as regular budgeting and tracking expenses, to maintain discipline.

3. Balancing Enjoyment and Frugality

Finding a balance between enjoying life and practicing frugality is essential:

- Mindful Enjoyment: Allow yourself to enjoy occasional splurges while keeping them within your budget.
- Value-Based Spending: Focus on spending money on experiences and items that truly enhance your quality of life.

Conclusion

Wealth is not always conspicuous, and many individuals achieve and maintain financial success through modest living, disciplined saving, and strategic investing. Understanding the principles of inconspicuous wealth can help individuals build long-term financial security and achieve their financial goals without succumbing to social pressures or unnecessary risks. This chapter has explored the habits, attitudes, and strategies of those who build and maintain wealth discreetly, highlighting the advantages of inconspicuous wealth. By adopting these principles, individuals can foster financial stability, flexibility, and freedom, ensuring a secure and prosperous future.

CHAPTER 19

REASONABLE IS GREATER THAN RATIONAL IN THE PSYCHOLOGY OF MONEY

In the realm of personal finance, decision-making often oscillates between what is considered rational and what is deemed reasonable. While traditional economic theories emphasize rationality, behavioral economics, and real-world experiences suggest that being reasonable often leads to better financial outcomes. This chapter explores why reasonable approaches, which consider human behavior and psychological factors, can be more effective than purely rational ones in managing money.

Understanding Rational and Reasonable

1. Rational Decision-Making

Rational decision-making is grounded in logic and objective analysis. It involves making choices that maximize utility based on available information. Characteristics of rational decision-making include:

- Maximization: Choosing the option that offers the highest expected return.
- Logical Analysis: Relying on data, statistics, and mathematical models to make decisions.
- Emotional Detachment: Minimizing the influence of emotions and biases.

2. Reasonable Decision-Making

Reasonable decision-making, on the other hand, acknowledges human limitations and the complexity of real-life situations. It involves making choices that are sensible and satisfactory within the context of personal circumstances. Characteristics of reasonable decision-making include:

- Satisficing: Opting for a satisfactory solution rather than the optimal one.
- Contextual Consideration: Taking into account personal values, emotions, and psychological factors.
- Practicality: Focusing on practical and achievable outcomes rather than theoretical perfection.

The Limitations of Rationality

1. Cognitive Biases

Even when attempting to be rational, individuals are prone to cognitive biases that can distort decision-making:

- Overconfidence: Believing in one's ability to predict market movements or financial outcomes more accurately than is realistic.

- Anchoring: Relying too heavily on the first piece of information encountered, such as the initial price of a stock.

2. Emotional Influence

Emotions play a significant role in financial decisions, often leading to irrational behavior:

- Fear and Greed: These emotions can drive market bubbles and crashes, influencing buying and selling decisions.

- Loss Aversion: The tendency to prefer avoiding losses over acquiring equivalent gains can lead to conservative investment strategies and reluctance to sell losing assets.

3. Complexity and Uncertainty

Financial markets and personal finances are complex and uncertain, making purely rational decision-making challenging:

- Information Overload: The sheer volume of financial data can overwhelm individuals, leading to analysis paralysis.

- Unpredictable Events: Market fluctuations, economic downturns, and personal emergencies are unpredictable, complicating rational planning.

The Advantages of Reasonableness

1. Human-Centric Approach

Reasonable decision-making embraces the human aspect of financial behavior:

- Emotional Intelligence: Recognizing and managing emotions can lead to more balanced and resilient financial decisions.
- Behavioral Adaptability: Being reasonable allows for flexibility and adaptation to changing circumstances and personal needs.

2. Simplicity and Practicality

Reasonable decisions often prioritize simplicity and practicality:

- Simplified Strategies: Simple financial strategies, such as automatic savings plans and diversified index funds, are easier to implement and maintain.
- Achievable Goals: Setting realistic and achievable financial goals fosters motivation and reduces stress.

3. Long-Term Perspective

Reasonable decision-making encourages a long-term perspective that aligns with overall well-being:

- Sustainable Habits: Focusing on sustainable financial habits, such as regular saving and prudent spending, promotes long-term financial health.

- Balanced Life: Balancing financial goals with personal values and quality of life ensures a holistic approach to financial well-being.

Examples of Reasonable Financial Decisions

1. Automatic Savings

Setting up automatic transfers to savings accounts ensures consistent savings without requiring continuous effort or decision-making:

- Ease of Implementation: Automatic savings plans simplify the process and help overcome procrastination.
- Behavioral Benefits: Automating savings leverages inertia, making it easier to accumulate wealth over time.

2. Diversified Investing

Investing in diversified portfolios, such as index funds, balances risk and return without the need for constant market analysis:

- Risk Management: Diversification reduces exposure to any single asset's volatility.
- Practicality: Index funds offer a simple and low-cost way to achieve market returns without extensive research.

3. Emergency Fund

Maintaining an emergency fund provides financial security and peace of mind:

- Preparedness: An emergency fund covers unexpected expenses, reducing the need for high-interest debt.

- Stability: Having a financial buffer contributes to overall financial stability and reduces stress.

Strategies for Embracing Reasonableness

1. Setting Realistic Goals

Setting realistic and achievable financial goals aligns with a reasonable approach:

- Specific and Measurable: Goals should be clear, specific, and measurable to track progress effectively.

- Incremental Progress: Breaking down larger goals into smaller, manageable steps fosters a sense of accomplishment.

2. Adopting a Balanced Approach

Balancing financial decisions with personal values and well-being promotes long-term satisfaction:

- Quality of Life: Considering the impact of financial decisions on overall quality of life ensures that money serves as a tool for achieving broader life goals.

- Holistic Planning: Integrating financial planning with other aspects of life, such as health and relationships, supports holistic well-being.

3. Leveraging Behavioral Insights

Applying behavioral insights can enhance financial decision-making:

- Nudging: Using small nudges, such as reminders and default options, can encourage positive financial behaviors.

- Behavioral Triggers: Identifying and managing triggers that lead to impulsive spending or poor financial decisions helps maintain discipline.

Real-World Implications

1. Financial Advising

Financial advisors can benefit from incorporating a reasonable approach when guiding clients:

- Personalization: Tailoring advice to clients' personal circumstances, values, and goals ensures that recommendations are practical and relevant.

- Emotional Support: Providing emotional support and addressing clients' psychological needs can enhance financial outcomes.

2. Policy Making

Policymakers can design financial regulations and programs that consider human behavior:

- Behavioral Interventions: Implementing policies that leverage behavioral insights, such as automatic enrollment in retirement plans, can improve financial well-being.

- Consumer Protection: Protecting consumers from predatory financial practices and ensuring access to clear information supports reasonable decision-making.

Conclusion

While rational decision-making is important, being reasonable often leads to better financial outcomes by acknowledging human behavior and psychological factors. Reasonable financial decisions are practical, adaptable, and aligned with personal values, promoting long-term financial stability and well-being. This chapter has explored the advantages of a reasonable approach over a purely rational one, highlighting strategies for embracing reasonableness in personal finance. By integrating these principles, individuals can make more balanced and effective financial decisions that support their overall quality of life.

CHAPTER 20

PAYING YOURSELF FIRST

"Paying yourself first" is a fundamental principle in personal finance that involves saving a predetermined portion of your income before allocating it for other expenses. This concept prioritizes savings and investment goals, ensuring that they are met before discretionary spending occurs. This chapter explores the importance of paying yourself first, various methods to implement it, and the long-term benefits of adopting this strategy.

The Concept of Paying Yourself First

1. Definition

Paying yourself first means setting aside a portion of your income for savings and investments before paying for other expenses. This approach ensures that financial goals are prioritized and met consistently.

2. Purpose

The primary purpose of paying yourself first is to build financial security and wealth over time. By making savings and investments a priority, individuals can ensure they are prepared for emergencies, achieve their financial goals, and secure their future.

Methods of Paying Yourself First

1. Employer-Sponsored Plans

One of the most effective ways to pay yourself first is through employer-sponsored retirement plans:

- 401(k) Plans: Contributing to a 401(k) plan allows employees to save a portion of their income before taxes, often with the benefit of employer matching contributions.
- Automatic Contributions: Setting up automatic contributions from each paycheck ensures consistent savings and takes advantage of compound growth over time.

2. Automatic Transfers

Automatic transfers from checking accounts to savings or investment accounts can help individuals pay themselves first without needing to remember to transfer money manually:

- Savings Accounts: Establishing an automatic transfer to a high-yield savings account can build an emergency fund or save for short-term goals.

- Investment Accounts: Regularly transferring money to investment accounts, such as IRAs or brokerage accounts, ensures long-term wealth accumulation.

3. Manual Transfers

For those who prefer a more hands-on approach, manual transfers can be scheduled regularly to ensure savings goals are met:

- Budgeting for Savings: Including savings as a line item in the monthly budget and manually transferring the allocated amount to savings or investment accounts.
- Consistency: Maintaining consistency in manual transfers helps reinforce the habit of paying yourself first.

Benefits of Paying Yourself First

1. Building an Emergency Fund

An emergency fund provides financial security and peace of mind by covering unexpected expenses:

- Financial Cushion: An emergency fund acts as a financial cushion, reducing the need to rely on credit cards or loans during emergencies.
- Stress Reduction: Knowing that funds are available for emergencies reduces financial stress and anxiety.

2. Achieving Financial Goals

Paying yourself first helps individuals achieve their short-term and long-term financial goals:

- Short-Term Goals: Saving for short-term goals, such as a vacation or a new car, becomes more manageable with consistent savings.

- Long-Term Goals: Regular contributions to retirement accounts and investment portfolios ensure that long-term goals, such as retirement and wealth building, are met.

3. Harnessing the Power of Compound Interest

Consistent saving and investing take advantage of compound interest, which significantly increases wealth over time:

- Compound Growth: The earlier and more consistently you save and invest, the more you benefit from the compound growth of your investments.

- Wealth Accumulation: Paying yourself first accelerates wealth accumulation by maximizing the time your money is invested and earning returns.

4. Encouraging Financial Discipline

Paying yourself first fosters financial discipline and healthy money management habits:

- Prioritizing Savings: By prioritizing savings over discretionary spending, individuals develop a mindset focused on financial security and responsibility.

- Budget Adherence: Allocating a portion of income to savings first encourages adherence to a budget and prevents overspending.

Strategies for Implementing Paying Yourself First

1. Determine Savings Goals

Setting clear savings goals is the first step in implementing the pay-yourself-first strategy:

- Specific Goals: Define specific savings goals, such as building an emergency fund, saving for a down payment on a house, or funding retirement.
- Prioritization: Prioritize goals based on importance and time horizon, focusing on building an emergency fund first, then contributing to retirement and other long-term goals.

2. Calculate the Savings Rate

Determine the appropriate savings rate based on income, expenses, and financial goals:

- Percentage of Income: A common recommendation is to save at least 20% of income, but this can vary based on individual circumstances and goals.
- Adjustments: Adjust the savings rate as needed to balance current financial needs with long-term goals.

3. Automate Savings

Automating savings ensures consistency and reduces the temptation to spend money before saving:

- Bank Transfers: Set up automatic transfers from checking to savings or investment accounts on payday.

- Payroll Deductions: Utilize employer options for automatic payroll deductions to retirement accounts.

4. Monitor and Adjust

Regularly monitor savings progress and adjust strategies as needed:

- Progress Tracking: Track progress toward savings goals using financial apps or spreadsheets.

- Adjustments: Adjust the savings rate or strategies based on changes in income, expenses, or financial goals.

Overcoming Common Challenges

1. Inconsistent Income

For individuals with inconsistent income, such as freelancers or gig workers, paying yourself first can be challenging:

- Variable Savings Rate: Set a variable savings rate based on a percentage of income rather than a fixed amount.

- Buffer Fund: Maintain a buffer fund to cover months with lower income and ensure consistent savings.

2. High Expenses

High living expenses can make it difficult to save consistently:

- Expense Reduction: Identify and reduce discretionary expenses to free up money for savings.

- Incremental Increases: Start with a small savings rate and gradually increase it as financial habits improve and expenses are managed.

3. Debt Repayment

Balancing debt repayment with savings goals can be challenging:

- Debt Prioritization: Focus on paying off high-interest debt while still allocating a portion of income to savings.

- Balanced Approach: Use a balanced approach, such as the 50/30/20 rule, to allocate income to needs, wants, and savings while addressing debt.

Real-World Examples

1. Employer-Sponsored Plans

Jane, a 30-year-old professional, contributes 10% of her salary to her 401(k) plan, with an additional 5% employer match. By paying herself first through automatic payroll deductions, she consistently builds her retirement savings and takes advantage of compound growth.

2. Automatic Transfers

John, a freelance graphic designer, sets up an automatic transfer of 20% of his monthly income to a high-yield savings account. This strategy ensures that he consistently saves for his financial goals, even with variable income.

3. Manual Transfers

Sarah, a teacher, manually transfers $500 from her checking account to her investment account each month. By including this transfer in her budget, she prioritizes her long-term financial goals and builds wealth over time.

Conclusion

Paying yourself first is a powerful strategy for achieving financial security and long-term wealth. By prioritizing savings and investments before other expenses, individuals can ensure that their financial goals are consistently met. This chapter has explored the concept of paying yourself first, various methods to implement it, and the benefits of adopting this strategy. By embracing this approach, individuals can build a solid financial foundation, achieve their goals, and secure their future.

CHAPTER 21

ZERO-BASE BUDGETING

Zero-based budgeting (ZBB) is a powerful financial management strategy that involves allocating every dollar of your expected income in advance, ensuring that no money is left unaccounted for. This budgeting system can be particularly effective for debt elimination, preventing overspending, and achieving financial goals. This chapter explores the principles of zero-based budgeting, its benefits, and practical steps to implement it successfully.

The Concept of Zero-Based Budgeting

1. Definition

Zero-based budgeting is a method where you plan and allocate your income to different spending categories and savings goals, ensuring that your total income minus your total expenses equals zero. Every dollar is assigned a specific purpose, eliminating any ambiguity about where your money is going.

2. Principle

The core principle of zero-based budgeting is to give every dollar a job. This approach helps you take control of your finances by ensuring that all income is purposefully directed towards expenses, savings, or debt repayment.

Benefits of Zero-Based Budgeting

1. Improved Financial Control

Zero-based budgeting provides a clear picture of your financial situation, allowing you to manage your money more effectively:

- Detailed Planning: By accounting for every dollar, you can make more informed spending decisions and avoid unnecessary expenses.
- Expense Tracking: Regularly tracking expenses against your budget helps identify areas where you might be overspending and allows for adjustments.

2. Debt Elimination

ZBB can be particularly effective for debt elimination:

- Prioritized Debt Repayment: By allocating a portion of your income specifically for debt repayment, you can systematically reduce your debt.

- Focused Approach: Zero-based budgeting helps you focus on debt repayment goals, ensuring that you make consistent progress.

3. Prevention of Overspending

ZBB helps prevent overspending by setting clear spending limits:

- Spending Discipline: Allocating money to specific categories helps you stick to your budget and avoid impulsive purchases.

- Awareness: Knowing exactly how much you can spend in each category increases awareness and promotes mindful spending.

4. Savings and Investment Goals

Zero-based budgeting supports the achievement of savings and investment goals:

- Automatic Savings: Allocating income to savings and investment accounts ensures that these goals are prioritized.

- Goal Achievement: By systematically saving and investing, you can achieve both short-term and long-term financial goals.

Steps to Implement Zero-Based Budgeting

1. Calculate Your Income

The first step in zero-based budgeting is to calculate your total expected income for the budgeting period:

- Regular Income: Include your salary, wages, and any other regular sources of income.
- Variable Income: Estimate any variable income, such as freelance work or side hustles, based on past averages.

2. List Your Expenses

List all your expected expenses for the budgeting period, categorizing them as necessary:

- Fixed Expenses: These are regular, recurring expenses such as rent, mortgage payments, utilities, and insurance.
- Variable Expenses: These include expenses that can fluctuate each month, such as groceries, transportation, and entertainment.
- Debt Repayment: Include payments for any outstanding debts, such as credit cards, student loans, and personal loans.
- Savings and Investments: Allocate money for savings accounts, emergency funds, and investment accounts.

3. Assign Every Dollar a Job

Allocate your total income to cover all listed expenses, ensuring that every dollar is assigned a specific purpose:

- Prioritization: Prioritize essential expenses, such as housing, utilities, and debt repayment, before allocating money to discretionary spending.
- Balanced Budget: Ensure that your total income minus your total expenses equals zero, meaning that all income is accounted for.

4. Track and Adjust

Regularly track your actual spending against your budget to ensure you stay on track:

- Expense Tracking: Use tools such as budgeting apps, spreadsheets, or financial journals to record and monitor your expenses.
- Adjustments: Make necessary adjustments to your budget as needed based on changes in income or unexpected expenses.

Practical Tips for Success

1. Use Budgeting Tools

Leverage budgeting tools and apps to simplify the zero-based budgeting process:

- Budgeting Apps: Apps like YNAB (You Need a Budget), Mint, and EveryDollar can help you create, track, and adjust your budget easily.

- Spreadsheets: Customized spreadsheets can provide a detailed view of your budget and allow for manual adjustments.

2. Stay Flexible

While zero-based budgeting requires careful planning, it's essential to remain flexible:

- Buffer Fund: Maintain a small buffer fund to cover minor unexpected expenses without disrupting your budget.
- Regular Reviews: Conduct regular budget reviews to adjust for changes in income, expenses, or financial goals.

3. Involve the Whole Family

If you share finances with a partner or family, involve everyone in the budgeting process:

- Collaborative Planning: Discuss financial goals and spending priorities together to ensure alignment and cooperation.
- Shared Responsibility: Assign specific budgeting tasks or categories to family members to promote accountability and participation.

4. Celebrate Milestones

Recognize and celebrate milestones and achievements in your budgeting journey:

- Progress Tracking: Track progress toward debt repayment, savings, and investment goals to stay motivated.

- Rewards: Reward yourself for reaching significant milestones, such as paying off a debt or reaching a savings goal, within your budget.

Real-World Examples

1. Debt Elimination

Emily, a recent college graduate, uses zero-based budgeting to tackle her student loans:

- Income Allocation: She allocates a portion of her monthly income specifically for debt repayment.

- Expense Tracking: By tracking her expenses, Emily identifies areas where she can cut back and reallocate funds to her loans.

- Progress: Over time, Emily has made significant progress in paying off her student loans and reducing her overall debt.

2. Saving for a Down Payment

John and Lisa, a young couple, use zero-based budgeting to save for a down payment on their first home:

- Income and Expenses: They calculate their combined income and list all monthly expenses.

- Savings Allocation: They allocate a portion of their income to a dedicated savings account for the down payment.

- Budget Adjustments: By adjusting their budget and cutting back on discretionary spending, John and Lisa accelerate their savings progress.

Conclusion

Zero-based budgeting is an effective financial management strategy that helps individuals take control of their finances, eliminate debt, prevent overspending, and achieve savings and investment goals. By allocating every dollar of income to specific purposes, individuals can ensure that their financial priorities are met and avoid unnecessary expenses. This chapter has explored the principles, benefits, and practical steps of zero-based budgeting, providing a comprehensive guide for implementing this powerful approach. By embracing zero-based budgeting, individuals can build a solid financial foundation, achieve their goals, and secure their financial future.

CHAPTER 22

THE 50/30/20 RULE

The 50/30/20 rule is a straightforward budgeting method that helps individuals manage their income by dividing it into three main categories: needs, wants, and savings. This approach simplifies budgeting by providing clear guidelines for spending and saving, making it easier to achieve financial stability and reach financial goals. This chapter explores the principles of the 50/30/20 rule, its benefits, and practical steps for implementing and adjusting it to fit individual financial situations.

The Concept of the 50/30/20 Rule

1. Definition

The 50/30/20 rule breaks down after-tax income into three categories:

- 50% for Needs: Essential expenses that are necessary for survival and maintaining a basic standard of living.

- 30% for Wants: Discretionary spending on non-essential items and activities that enhance quality of life.

- 20% for Savings and Debt Repayment: Allocating income towards savings, investments, and paying off debt.

2. Purpose

The primary purpose of the 50/30/20 rule is to provide a balanced approach to budgeting that ensures essential needs are met, allows for enjoyable spending, and prioritizes financial goals such as saving and debt reduction.

Benefits of the 50/30/20 Rule

1. Simplicity and Clarity

The 50/30/20 rule offers a simple and clear framework for managing finances:

- Easy to Understand: The percentages are easy to remember and apply, making budgeting less complicated.

- Clear Priorities: By categorizing expenses, individuals can easily see where their money is going and make adjustments as needed.

2. Balanced Financial Management

This rule promotes balanced financial management by addressing essential needs, allowing for discretionary spending, and prioritizing savings:

- Meeting Needs: Ensures that essential expenses are covered, providing financial security.

- Enjoyable Spending: Allows for discretionary spending, enhancing the quality of life without compromising financial stability.

- Financial Goals: Emphasizes the importance of saving and debt repayment, fostering long-term financial health.

3. Flexibility

The 50/30/20 rule can be adjusted to fit individual financial situations and goals:

- Customizable: The percentages can be modified based on income level and financial obligations, making it adaptable to different circumstances.

- Scalable: Suitable for various income levels, from entry-level earners to high-income individuals.

Implementing the 50/30/20 Rule

1. Calculate After-Tax Income

The first step is to determine your total monthly after-tax income:

- Net Income: Include your salary, wages, and any other sources of regular income, after taxes and deductions.

2. Categorize Expenses

Next, categorize your monthly expenses into needs, wants, and savings:

- Needs (50%): Essential expenses such as rent or mortgage, utilities, groceries, transportation, insurance, and minimum debt payments.

- Wants (30%): Discretionary spending on items such as dining out, entertainment, hobbies, travel, and non-essential shopping.

- Savings and Debt Repayment (20%): Contributions to savings accounts, retirement funds, investments, and additional debt repayments.

3. Allocate Income

Allocate your after-tax income according to the 50/30/20 rule:

- Needs: Allocate 50% of your income to cover essential expenses.

- Wants: Allocate 30% of your income for discretionary spending.

- Savings and Debt Repayment: Allocate 20% of your income towards savings and debt repayment.

4. Track and Adjust

Regularly track your spending to ensure it aligns with your budget and make adjustments as needed:

- Expense Tracking: Use budgeting apps, spreadsheets, or financial journals to monitor expenses.

- Adjustments: Adjust the percentages if your needs exceed 50% of your income or if you want to save more aggressively.

Adjusting the 50/30/20 Rule

1. Higher Needs Expenses

If your needs account for more than 50% of your income, adjust the percentages accordingly:

- Increased Needs: Allocate a higher percentage, such as 60% or 70%, to cover essential expenses.

- Reduced Wants or Savings: Reduce the allocation for wants or savings to balance the budget.

2. Aggressive Saving Goals

If you have aggressive saving goals or significant debt to repay, you may choose to allocate more than 20% of your income to savings and debt repayment:

- Increased Savings: Allocate a higher percentage, such as 25% or 30%, towards savings and debt repayment.

- Reduced Wants: Decrease the allocation for wants to accommodate the increased savings rate.

3. Variable Income

For individuals with variable income, such as freelancers or gig workers, adjusting the 50/30/20 rule can help manage fluctuations:

- Average Income: Calculate an average monthly income based on past earnings to set a baseline for budgeting.

- Buffer Fund: Maintain a buffer fund to cover months with lower income and ensure consistent savings and expense coverage.

Practical Tips for Success

1. Use Budgeting Tools

Leverage budgeting tools and apps to simplify the implementation of the 50/30/20 rule:

- Budgeting Apps: Apps like Mint, YNAB, and EveryDollar can help create, track, and adjust your budget.

- Spreadsheets: Customized spreadsheets can provide a detailed view of your budget and allow for manual adjustments.

2. Stay Flexible

While the 50/30/20 rule provides a general guideline, it's important to remain flexible and adjust as needed:

- Regular Reviews: Conduct regular budget reviews to assess your spending and make necessary adjustments.

- Adaptability: Be open to modifying the percentages based on changes in income, expenses, or financial goals.

3. Involve the Whole Family

If you share finances with a partner or family, involve everyone in the budgeting process:

- Collaborative Planning: Discuss financial goals and spending priorities together to ensure alignment and cooperation.

- Shared Responsibility: Assign specific budgeting tasks or categories to family members to promote accountability and participation.

4. Celebrate Milestones

Recognize and celebrate milestones and achievements in your budgeting journey:

- Progress Tracking: Track progress towards savings, debt repayment, and other financial goals to stay motivated.

- Rewards: Reward yourself for reaching significant milestones, such as paying off a debt or reaching a savings goal, within your budget.

Real-World Examples

1. Young Professional

Alex, a young professional, uses the 50/30/20 rule to manage his finances:

- Income Allocation: He allocates 50% of his after-tax income to cover rent, utilities, groceries, and transportation.
- Discretionary Spending: He allocates 30% for dining out, entertainment, and hobbies.
- Savings: He allocates 20% to his emergency fund and retirement account, ensuring he is building a solid financial foundation.

2. Family with Children

Sarah and Mark, a couple with two children, adjust the 50/30/20 rule to fit their higher needs expenses:

- Adjusted Needs: They allocate 60% of their income to cover mortgage payments, utilities, groceries, childcare, and insurance.
- Reduced Wants: They allocate 20% for discretionary spending on family activities and vacations.
- Savings and Debt Repayment: They allocate 20% to savings and debt repayment, prioritizing their financial security.

3. Freelancer

Emily, a freelance graphic designer, adapts the 50/30/20 rule to manage her variable income:

- Average Income: She calculates an average monthly income based on her past earnings.

- Buffer Fund: She maintains a buffer fund to cover months with lower income.

- Flexible Allocation: She adjusts the percentages based on her income fluctuations, ensuring she consistently saves and covers her expenses.

Conclusion

The 50/30/20 rule is a practical and balanced budgeting method that helps individuals manage their income effectively by dividing it into three main categories: needs, wants, and savings. By providing clear guidelines for spending and saving, this approach simplifies budgeting and promotes financial stability. This chapter has explored the principles, benefits, and practical steps for implementing the 50/30/20 rule, along with tips for adjusting it to fit individual financial situations. By adopting this method, individuals can achieve their financial goals, maintain a balanced lifestyle, and secure their financial future.

CHAPTER 23

DO YOU HAVE A SCARCITY MINDSET OR AN ABUNDANCE MINDSET?

The mindset with which you approach your finances and life in general can significantly influence your behavior, decisions, and overall well-being. A scarcity mindset and an abundance mindset represent two opposing ways of thinking about resources and opportunities. Understanding these mindsets and identifying which one you align with can help you make more informed choices and improve your financial and personal life. This chapter explores the characteristics of scarcity and abundance mindsets, their impact on behavior, and strategies for cultivating an abundance mindset.

Understanding the Scarcity Mindset

1. Definition

A scarcity mindset is characterized by the perception of lack. Individuals with this mindset believe that there aren't enough resources, opportunities, or wealth to go around. This belief can manifest in various ways, leading to feelings of competition, fear, and insecurity.

2. Characteristics

Common characteristics of a scarcity mindset include:

- Fear of Loss: A constant worry about losing what you have, leading to risk-averse behavior.

- Zero-Sum Thinking: Believing that one person's gain is another person's loss, resulting in competitive and protective behaviors.

- Short-Term Focus: Emphasizing immediate needs and short-term goals over long-term planning.

- Hoarding Behavior: Accumulating resources excessively to prevent others from accessing them.

3. Examples of Scarcity Mindset

- Financial Insecurity: Constantly worrying about money and fearing that you will never have enough to meet your needs.

- Job Competition: Believing that there are limited career opportunities and that you must outdo others to succeed.

- Social Comparisons: Frequently comparing yourself to others and feeling envious or threatened by their success.

Impact of a Scarcity Mindset

1. On Financial Behavior

A scarcity mindset can lead to detrimental financial behaviors:

- Impulsive Spending: Responding to artificial scarcity tactics in sales and marketing, leading to impulsive purchases and financial strain.
- Underinvestment: Fearing loss and avoiding investment opportunities that could grow wealth over time.
- Debt Accumulation: Using credit to satisfy immediate desires rather than saving and planning for future needs.

2. On Personal Well-Being

The psychological impact of a scarcity mindset can be profound:

- Stress and Anxiety: Constant worry about not having enough can lead to chronic stress and anxiety.
- Relationship Strain: Competitive and protective behaviors can strain relationships with friends, family, and colleagues.

- Limited Growth: A focus on short-term needs and fears can prevent personal and professional growth.

Understanding the Abundance Mindset

1. Definition

An abundance mindset is characterized by the belief that there are enough resources, opportunities, and wealth to go around. Individuals with this mindset view the world as a place of plenty, where everyone can succeed and prosper.

2. Characteristics

Common characteristics of an abundance mindset include:

- Optimism: A positive outlook on life and the belief that good things are possible.
- Collaborative Thinking: Believing in win-win situations and seeking collaborative opportunities.
- Long-Term Focus: Emphasizing long-term goals and planning for future success.
- Generosity: Sharing resources and opportunities with others without fear of losing out.

3. Examples of Abundance Mindset

- Financial Confidence: Believing that you can always find ways to earn and save money, leading to prudent financial management.

- Career Growth: Viewing challenges as opportunities for growth and believing that there are enough career opportunities for everyone.

- Celebrating Others' Success: Feeling genuinely happy for others' achievements and using them as inspiration for your own growth.

Impact of an Abundance Mindset

1. On Financial Behavior

An abundance mindset can lead to positive financial behaviors:

- Prudent Spending: Making thoughtful purchases based on value and need, rather than succumbing to artificial scarcity.

- Investment and Growth: Taking calculated risks and investing in opportunities that can grow wealth over time.

- Debt Avoidance: Prioritizing savings and investments over unnecessary spending, leading to financial stability.

2. On Personal Well-Being

The psychological impact of an abundance mindset is generally positive:

- Reduced Stress: A belief in abundance reduces financial anxiety and promotes a sense of security.

- Healthy Relationships: Collaborative and generous behaviors strengthen relationships with others.

- Personal Growth: A focus on long-term goals and continuous improvement fosters personal and professional development.

Artificial Scarcity in Marketing

1. Tactics Used

Marketers often use artificial scarcity to drive sales and create urgency:

- Limited-Time Offers: Promoting products as available for a limited time to encourage immediate purchases.

- Exclusive Access: Creating a sense of exclusivity by limiting access to products or services.

- Countdown Timers: Using countdown timers on websites to pressure customers into making quick decisions.

2. Psychological Effects

Artificial scarcity can trigger a fear of missing out (FOMO) and prompt impulsive spending:

- Urgency and Panic: The perception of limited availability can create a sense of urgency and panic, leading to hasty decisions.

- Herd Behavior: Seeing others rush to buy can reinforce the belief that the opportunity is scarce and valuable.

3. Real-World Consequences

Artificial scarcity has led to significant real-world consequences:

- Black Friday Incidents: Sales events with limited offers have historically resulted in injuries and even deaths as shoppers compete aggressively.
- Product Shortages: Artificial scarcity can create false demand, leading to actual shortages and inflated prices.

Cultivating an Abundance Mindset

1. Shift Your Perspective

Changing your mindset from scarcity to abundance involves a deliberate shift in perspective:

- Focus on Possibilities: Concentrate on opportunities and possibilities rather than limitations and obstacles.
- Practice Gratitude: Regularly acknowledging and appreciating what you have can foster a sense of abundance.

2. Set Long-Term Goals

Setting long-term goals helps to shift focus from immediate needs to future possibilities:

- Vision Planning: Create a vision for your future and set specific, achievable goals to work towards it.
- Continuous Learning: Invest in personal and professional development to expand your opportunities.

3. Build Collaborative Relationships

Cultivating collaborative relationships reinforces the belief in abundance:

- Networking: Build a supportive network of like-minded individuals who share your values and goals.
- Mentorship: Seek mentors who can guide you and offer perspectives on achieving abundance.

4. Embrace Generosity

Practicing generosity can reinforce an abundance mindset:

- Giving Back: Share your resources and opportunities with others through charitable donations, volunteering, or mentoring.
- Celebrate Others: Celebrate the success of others and find joy in their achievements.

Practical Steps to Overcome a Scarcity Mindset

1. Identify Limiting Beliefs

Recognize and challenge the limiting beliefs that contribute to a scarcity mindset:

- Self-Reflection: Reflect on your thoughts and behaviors to identify patterns of scarcity thinking.
- Cognitive Reframing: Reframe negative thoughts into positive affirmations that promote abundance.

2. Budget and Plan

Create a budget and financial plan that supports an abundance mindset:

- Savings and Investments: Prioritize savings and investments to build financial security and growth.

- Mindful Spending: Make spending decisions based on value and long-term benefits rather than fear of scarcity.

3. Seek Professional Help

Consider seeking professional help to address deeply ingrained scarcity thinking:

- Therapy and Counseling: Work with a therapist or counselor to explore and address underlying issues related to scarcity.

- Financial Coaching: Engage a financial coach to develop strategies for building an abundance mindset and achieving financial goals.

Conclusion

A scarcity mindset and an abundance mindset represent two fundamentally different approaches to life and finances. While a scarcity mindset focuses on lack and competition, an abundance mindset emphasizes possibilities, collaboration, and long-term growth. Understanding these mindsets and actively working to cultivate an abundance mindset can lead to better financial behaviors, improved well-being, and greater overall satisfaction. This chapter has explored the characteristics and impacts of both mindsets, strategies for overcoming a scarcity mindset, and practical steps for embracing an abundance mindset. By shifting your perspective and adopting an abundance mindset, you can create a more fulfilling and prosperous life.

CONCLUSION

Understanding the psychology of money is fundamental to achieving personal and societal financial health. Throughout this book, we have explored various aspects of financial behavior, from budgeting strategies and mindsets to the impact of emotions and cognitive biases on financial decisions. This final chapter summarizes the key insights discussed and reinforces the importance of recognizing and addressing the psychological factors that influence our financial lives.

Key Insights

1. The Importance of Financial Mindsets

One of the recurring themes in this book is the significant impact of financial mindsets on behavior and outcomes. Whether you possess a scarcity mindset or an abundance mindset can shape how you approach saving, spending, and investing. Cultivating an abundance mindset encourages optimism, generosity, and long-term planning, which are crucial for financial success and well-being.

2. Effective Budgeting Strategies

We explored several budgeting strategies, including zero-based budgeting and the 50/30/20 rule. Each method provides a structured approach to managing income, expenses, and savings. Zero-based budgeting ensures every dollar is accounted for, promoting disciplined spending and savings habits. The 50/30/20 rule offers a balanced approach, allocating income to needs, wants, and savings, and can be adjusted to fit individual circumstances.

3. Emotional and Cognitive Influences

Emotions and cognitive biases play a pivotal role in financial decision-making. Fear, greed, overconfidence, and loss aversion can lead to impulsive decisions and suboptimal financial outcomes. Recognizing these influences allows individuals to make more informed and rational choices, improving their financial health.

4. The Role of Financial Education

Financial education is essential for empowering individuals to make informed decisions. Understanding basic financial concepts, such as budgeting, saving, investing, and debt management, provides a solid foundation for achieving financial goals. Continuous learning and seeking professional advice further enhance financial literacy and decision-making.

5. The Impact of Social and Cultural Factors

Social and cultural factors significantly shape financial behavior. Family background, societal norms, and cultural values influence attitudes toward money, spending, saving, and investing. Recognizing these influences helps individuals make conscious financial choices aligned with their values and goals.

6. The Power of Automation

Automating savings and investments simplifies financial management and ensures consistent progress toward goals. Automatic transfers to savings and investment accounts take advantage of inertia, making it easier to build wealth over time. This approach also reduces the temptation to spend impulsively and reinforces disciplined financial habits.

7. The Benefits of Long-Term Planning

Long-term financial planning is crucial for building and maintaining wealth. Setting clear financial goals, creating a budget, and investing for the future provide a roadmap for financial success. Long-term planning also helps individuals navigate economic uncertainties and achieve financial stability.

8. Overcoming Debt and Building Wealth

Effective debt management strategies, such as prioritizing high-interest debt and adopting a balanced approach to saving and debt repayment, are essential for financial health. Building an emergency fund, investing for growth, and practicing prudent spending habits contribute to long-term wealth accumulation and financial security.

9. The Role of Technology

Advancements in technology, such as fintech solutions, AI, and blockchain, are transforming financial behavior and decision-making. These innovations provide accessible, convenient, and personalized financial services, empowering individuals to manage their finances more effectively. Embracing technology can enhance financial literacy, streamline budgeting, and support better investment decisions.

Implications for Personal and Societal Financial Health

1. Personal Financial Health

Understanding the psychology of money enables individuals to make more informed and rational financial decisions. By recognizing and addressing emotional and cognitive influences, adopting effective budgeting strategies, and embracing long-term planning, individuals can achieve financial stability, reduce stress, and improve overall well-being. Cultivating an abundance mindset and leveraging technology further enhance personal financial health.

2. Societal Financial Health

At a societal level, promoting financial education and literacy is essential for economic stability and growth. Policymakers, educators, and financial institutions play a crucial role in providing accessible financial education and resources. Encouraging responsible financial behavior, protecting consumers from predatory practices, and leveraging technology to promote financial inclusion contribute to a healthier and more resilient economy.

Conclusion

The psychology of money encompasses a wide range of factors that influence financial behavior and decision-making. By understanding these factors, individuals can develop healthier financial habits, achieve their goals, and secure their future. This book has provided insights into various aspects of financial psychology, from mindsets and emotions to budgeting strategies and technological advancements. By applying these insights, individuals can take control of their financial lives, fostering both personal and societal financial health.

As we conclude this journey through the psychology of money, remember that financial well-being is not just about numbers and dollars. It is about understanding the underlying psychological influences, making informed choices, and cultivating a mindset that promotes growth, security, and fulfillment. By embracing these principles, you can navigate the complexities of the financial world with confidence and achieve lasting financial success.

REFERENCES

Books

1. Ariely, Dan. Predictably Irrational: The Hidden Forces That Shape Our Decisions. HarperCollins, 2008.

2. Belsky, Gary, and Thomas Gilovich. Why Smart People Make Big Money Mistakes and How to Correct Them: Lessons from the Life-Changing Science of Behavioral Economics. Simon & Schuster, 2010.

3. Kahneman, Daniel. Thinking, Fast and Slow. Farrar, Straus and Giroux, 2011.

4. Malkiel, Burton G. A Random Walk Down Wall Street: The Time-Tested Strategy for Successful Investing. W.W. Norton & Company, 2015.

5. Sethi, Ramit. I Will Teach You to Be Rich. Workman Publishing Company, 2009.

6. Stanley, Thomas J., and William D. Danko. The Millionaire Next Door: The Surprising Secrets of America's Wealthy. Taylor Trade Publishing, 1996.

7. Thaler, Richard H., and Cass R. Sunstein. Nudge: Improving Decisions About Health, Wealth, and Happiness. Penguin Books, 2008.

Academic Papers and Articles

1. Deaton, Angus, and Daniel Kahneman. "High income improves evaluation of life but not emotional well-being." Proceedings of the National Academy of Sciences, vol. 107, no. 38, 2010, pp. 16489-16493.

2. Mischel, Walter, Ebbe B. Ebbesen, and Antonette Raskoff Zeiss. "Cognitive and attentional mechanisms in delay of gratification." Journal of Personality and Social Psychology, vol. 21, no. 2, 1972, pp. 204-218.

3. Thaler, Richard H. "Mental accounting and consumer choice." Marketing Science, vol. 4, no. 3, 1985, pp. 199-214.

Websites and Online Resources

1. Bogleheads. Investing Advice Inspired by John Bogle. https://www.bogleheads.org

2. Investopedia. Financial Education Resources. https://www.investopedia.com

3. Mint. Personal Finance Tools and Resources. https://www.mint.com

4. NerdWallet. Financial Advice and Tools. https://www.nerdwallet.com

Reports and White Papers

1. Board of Governors of the Federal Reserve System. Report on the Economic Well-Being of U.S. Households in 2020. https://www.federalreserve.gov/publications/2021-economic-well-being-of-us-households-in-2020-executive-summary.htm

2. FINRA Investor Education Foundation. National Financial Capability Study. https://www.usfinancialcapability.org

Recommended Further Reading

1. Chatzky, Jean. Make Money, Not Excuses: Wake Up, Take Charge, and Overcome Your Financial Fears Forever. Crown Business, 2008.

2. Collins, Chuck, and Felice Yeskel. Economic Apartheid in America: A Primer on Economic Inequality and Insecurity. The New Press, 2005.

3. Orman, Suze. The Money Book for the Young, Fabulous & Broke. Riverhead Trade, 2005.

4. Robbins, Tony. Money: Master the Game: 7 Simple Steps to Financial Freedom. Simon & Schuster, 2014.

5. Schiff, Peter D. The Little Book of Bull Moves, Updated and Expanded: How to Keep Your Portfolio Up When the Market Is Up, Down, or Sideways. Wiley, 2010.

Conclusion

This comprehensive list of references and further reading materials offers a solid foundation for those interested in delving deeper into the topics discussed in this book. By exploring these resources, readers can expand their understanding of the psychology of money, financial behavior, and effective money management strategies. Whether you are a novice or an experienced financial enthusiast, these references provide valuable insights to help you achieve financial well-being and success.

www.ingramcontent.com/pod-product-compliance
Lightning Source LLC
LaVergne TN
LVHW052321200926
848481LV00002B/631

* 9 7 9 8 3 3 0 4 9 1 4 2 1 *